T0288285

CONCISE
LINCOLN
LIBRARY

—

EDITED BY RICHARD W. ETULAIN

AND SYLVIA FRANK RODRIGUE

JAMES TACKACH

Lincoln and the Natural Environment

Southern Illinois University Press
Carbondale

Southern Illinois University Press
www.siupress.com

22 21 20 19   4 3 2 1

The Concise Lincoln Library has been made possible
in part through a generous donation by the Leland
E. and LaRita R. Boren Trust.
   Volumes in this series have been published with
support from the Abraham Lincoln Bicentennial
Foundation, dedicated to perpetuating and expand-
ing Lincoln's vision for America and completing
America's unfinished work.

Jacket illustration adapted from a painting by
Wendy Allen

Library of Congress Cataloging-in-Publication Data
Names: Tackach, James, author.
Title: Lincoln and the natural environment /
James Tackach.
Description: Carbondale, IL : Southern Illinois Uni-
versity Press, [2019] | Series: Concise Lincoln library
| Includes bibliographical references and index.
Identifiers: LCCN 2018011325 | ISBN 9780809336982
(cloth : alk. paper) | ISBN 9780809336999 (e-book)
Subjects: LCSH: Lincoln, Abraham, 1809–1865. |
Human ecology—United States—History—
19th century. | United States—Environmental
conditions—History. | Environmentalism—
United States—History.
Classification: LCC E457.2 .T125 2019 | DDC
973.7092—dc23 LC record available at
https://lccn.loc.gov/2018011325

CONTENTS

ILLUSTRATIONS

LINCOLN AND THE NATURAL ENVIRONMENT

INTRODUCTION

A braham Lincoln's lifetime spanned a remarkable period in American environmental history. He was born in 1809, when most of his countrymen and countrywomen lived and worked on farms, directly connected to and dependent on the American natural landscape in their everyday lives. Agriculture was indeed the nation's main economic activity. At about the time of Lincoln's birth, however, a gradual migration away from farming was commencing, as large numbers of Americans were moving to towns and cities and making their living in the new economy ushered in by the Industrial Revolution. During the early decades of the nineteenth century, American mills and factories began to appear and produce metals and consumer products—textiles and clothing, tools, farm equipment, household products—previously crafted laboriously by hand or imported from abroad. Americans who worked in these industries lived not on farms but in mill and factory towns and in rapidly growing cities. Immigrants coming to the United States in the early decades of the nineteenth century, most of whom lacked the money to buy land for farming, settled in cities and towns and sought work in the new industrial economy. Throughout the first half of the nineteenth century, most Americans continued to live on farms and in small communities, but an economic shift and accompanying lifestyle changes had begun.

The Industrial Revolution sparked a transportation revolution. The steam engine, developed in the final decades of the eighteenth century, was adapted for use on ships two years before Lincoln's birth, enabling them to travel upstream against the current and cross wide bodies of water much faster than vessels powered by sails and oars. The great symbol of the new industrial order, the locomotive, appeared while Lincoln was a teenager, and railroad networks spread rapidly across the United States during his young adulthood. Trains greatly reduced travel time for passengers and transportation time for products between sections of the rapidly expanding United States. Machines—the cotton gin, the reaper—also came to America's farms. The Industrial Revolution, during and after Lincoln's lifetime, transformed the U.S. economy and social and cultural landscapes, and it also reshaped the nation's natural environment in significant ways.

Lincoln served as president during the Civil War, the most devastating war in U.S. history, in which more than seven hundred thousand Americans died from battle wounds or disease. The brutal four-year conflict also caused significant infrastructure and environmental damage in the South, where most of the fighting and troops movements took place. Cities and towns were burned, and plantations, farms, and natural landscapes were seriously damaged and destroyed in the North's effort to subdue the rebellious South. To heal the nation's wounds of war, postwar reconstruction would have to be spiritual, political, economic, and environmental. When Lincoln stated in his Second Inaugural Address that he and his fellow citizens needed "to bind up the nation's wounds,"[1] he was likely aware that the nation's natural landscape had suffered greatly during the conflict and would need attention and care after the fighting ended.

During Lincoln's lifetime, even before the Civil War, the first American voices for environmental protection and conservation were heard. The industrialization of the nation sparked a backlash from individuals—Henry David Thoreau, William Cullen Bryant, George Catlin, Thomas Cole, Frederick Law Olmsted, George Perkins Marsh—who contended that America's natural resources, green landscapes, and natural beauty were being seriously threatened by the new industrial forces. Before the Industrial Revolution, and probably during its early stages, most Americans reasoned that their broad continent was a land of boundless natural beauty and bounty. The country's forests extended indefinitely; its wildlife, fish, and fowl were and would remain plentiful; its soils would remain forever fertile. But Lincoln witnessed America's forests begin to disappear at a rapid rate as wood was devoured for construction and fuel, and wildlife was significantly diminished as a result of deforestation. Forests were further depleted as Civil War armies moved through natural land-scapes and waged war with modern weaponry.

Deforestation was only one of many environmental wounds suf-fered by the nation in Lincoln's lifetime. Unfertilized soils became depleted and infertile after several growing seasons. Rivers were dammed to create water power to run mills and factories, altering and blocking fish migrations, and the runoff from the mills and factories often polluted rivers. Whales, hunted in the late eighteenth and early nineteenth centuries as a source of desperately needed fuel oil, vir-tually disappeared from the Atlantic coastal waters where they had once been plentiful. Writers like Bryant and Thoreau tried to draw the public's and the government's attention to the wounds that the natural landscape suffered as the nation embraced industrialization.

An environmental biography of Lincoln would reveal a man whose relationship with the natural environment was complicated and prob-lematic, but also evolving, even at the time of his death. Lincoln was born on a frontier family farm and lived and worked on family farms through his young adulthood, but he gradually grew unenthusiastic about the arduous labor required by a life so close to and dependent on the land. He also realized how vulnerable most farmers were to environmental forces; foul weather could destroy a season's entire crop and plunge a farm family into starvation. Lincoln's biological mother died when he was nine years old from an environmental disease, milk sickness. Moreover, the subsistence farming that his family practiced offered an ambitious young man like Lincoln little opportunity for upward social, economic, or intellectual mobility. Lincoln left farming and the frontier at age twenty-two, never to return. As an adult, he embraced town and city life and had no desire to go back to rural America. He left farming and other oc-cupations closely connected to the natural environment—piloting flatboats, surveying land—eventually choosing law as his profession and entering politics. He would earn his living with books in offices, not in the fields with ax and plow.

Early in his political life, Lincoln became an avid advocate for the new industrial and technological order that was taking hold in the United States in the middle of the nineteenth century. He spoke enthusiastically of the railroad, the steamboat, and other machines that were transforming the United States from a nation of farmers to an industrial power. He held a lifelong interest in machines and inventions and offered lectures about them. He earned a patent for a device to enable boats to pass through shallow waters. Lincoln's first political party affiliation, during the 1830s, was with the Whigs, whose main platform planks included support for "internal improvements," the construction of canals, bridges, harbors, dams, roads, and railroads to facilitate the efficient transportation of manufactured goods to American consumers living in a geographically expanding nation. Many of these internal improvements were designed to master the natural environment—to dam and redirect rivers, to connect waterways via canals, for example. Lincoln's Whigs also supported high tariffs on imported manufactured goods to protect American manufacturers from foreign competition and thereby encourage American consumers to purchase American-made products. The Whigs put forth no environmental agenda, no policies to protect the natural environment as the nation experienced and embraced the Industrial Revolution.

As president, however, Lincoln, though preoccupied by the war, signed some environmentally progressive legislation, including the unprecedented Yosemite Valley Grant Act, which preserved land in California's Yosemite Valley from development, and he approved the bill that reorganized the Department of Agriculture, giving it a more prominent position in the federal government. He also signed legislation creating the nation's land grant colleges, which would offer programs in the academic study of agriculture and engineering. He signed the Homestead Act, which was designed to offer inexpensive land grants to small farmers. Throughout his political career, often to great effect, Lincoln used imagery, metaphors, and analogies drawn from the natural world of his youth and young adulthood. Farm fields, crops, fish, and animals appeared frequently in his stories, writings, and speeches. His best-known speech, the Gettysburg Address, moved to the rhythms of the natural world: birth, death, and rebirth. Lincoln appreciated and enjoyed places of natural beauty, such as Niagara Falls and Soldiers' Home outside of urban Washington, which became his summer White House. His reading also took him vicariously into the natural world; he enjoyed nature poetry and narratives by travel writers who explored the unsettled regions of the United States.

Lists of the most environmentally friendly U.S. presidents, however, do not consistently include Lincoln. In 2012, Corporate Knights, a media and financial services company that endorses "clean capitalism" for businesses and corporations, surveyed twelve leading environmental groups—organizations such as the Sierra Club and Worldwatch Institute—and then used those survey results to rank U.S. presidents in terms of their commitment to a healthy natural environment. Predictably, Theodore Roosevelt, a lifelong outdoorsman, ranked first on the list; he created wildlife refuges, forest preserves, and national parks during his presidency, and he authored books such as *Hunting Trips of a Ranchman* and *The Wilderness Hunter.* Ranking second on the Corporate Knights' list of environmentally sensitive presidents was Richard Nixon. Not known as an avid outdoorsman, Nixon, nonetheless, created the U.S. Environmental Protection Agency to monitor and protect the country's natural environment and signed the landmark Clean Water Act, the Marine Mammal Protection Act, and other environmental legislation. Ranking third was Jimmy Carter, an avid fly fisherman and former peanut farmer, who as president protected lands in Alaska from commercial development and continually urged Americans to conserve energy and thereby reduce their dependence on fossil fuels. Carter had solar panels installed on the White House, and during the Arab oil embargo of the late 1970s, he gave a television address to the nation dressed in a sweater, instead of the traditional suit jacket, to dramatize the need for Americans to turn down their home thermostats and thereby save energy and reduce their dependence on fuel oil. Only five additional presidents received votes in the Corporate Knights' survey of environmentally friendly U.S. presidents, in the following order: Barack Obama, Thomas Jefferson, Gerald Ford, Franklin Roosevelt, and Bill Clinton.[2] Lincoln did not appear on the Corporate Knights' list.

In 2011, Mother Nature Network, a website devoted to environmental sustainability, listed six "eco-friendly" U.S. presidents in this ranked order: Jefferson, for his commitment to the American landscape; Theodore Roosevelt; Franklin Roosevelt, for creating the Civilian Conservation Corps during the Great Depression; Lyndon Johnson, for signing landmark legislation such as the Clean Air Act of 1963, the Wilderness Act of 1964, and the Endangered Species Act of 1966; Nixon; and Carter.[3] In 2009, the Autonomie Project, a Boston-based fashion company devoted to fair trade and environmentally friendly methods of producing clothing and fashion accessories, rated U.S. presidents on the basis of their commitment to a healthy natural environment, listing those with the best and the worst environmental records. The Autonomie Project's top four green presidents were Teddy Roosevelt, Carter, Nixon, and Woodrow Wilson, who established the National Park Service. Other presidents included on the green list were Jefferson, Bill Clinton, Franklin Roosevelt, Lincoln, Lyndon Johnson, and John Kennedy.[4] Lincoln received a positive ranking mainly for his signing of the Yosemite Valley Grant Act. In 2009, an article by Brian Merchant on *TreeHugger*, an online media outlet dedicated to sustainability, ranked Lincoln number three on its list of the greenest American presidents, also citing his signing of the Yosemite Valley Grant Act as the main reason for his high ranking.[5]

Environmental historians have also analyzed and judged U.S. presidents in terms of their commitment to the natural environment. In his 2015 book, *Presidents and the American Environment*, Otis L. Graham Jr. contends that Benjamin Harrison, the twenty-third U.S. president, whose term of office ran from 1889 through 1893, was the first president to develop an environmental agenda. Harrison signed into law the General Revision Act of 1891, which included, buried within its pages, a Forest Reserve Act to protect American woodlands from commercial use and development. Graham devotes full chapters in his book to Theodore Roosevelt and to Franklin Roosevelt. Graham lumps together Lyndon Johnson, Richard Nixon, Gerald Ford, and Jimmy Carter in a chapter titled "Environmentalism Arrives, 1960s–1970s." Graham also includes chapters on presidents after Harrison who lacked any environmental agenda, and he specifically identifies Ronald Reagan, a rancher and horseman, as being unfriendly to the natural environment. During his tenure in the White House, President Reagan, a staunch climate change denier, removed the solar panels that President Carter had installed. (President Obama had them reinstalled.) Lincoln, like all presidents who served before Harrison, receives only passing commentary in Graham's book. Graham acknowledges that Lincoln signed the Yosemite Valley Grant Act but notes that Lincoln left no comment on his action, suggesting that Lincoln likely considered the act of little importance.[6]

In *The Republic of Nature: An Environmental History of the United States*, published in 2012, Mark Fiege devotes many pages to Lincoln, focusing on his relationship with the land—his break from a life of farming, his attempts to master the natural environment with internal improvement projects, and the environmental devastation wrought by the Civil War. Olivier Fraysse's 1988 *Lincoln, Land, and Labor* discusses Lincoln's land and agricultural policies. Neither Fiege nor Fraysse ranks U.S. presidents as stewards of the natural environment, nor do they award Lincoln a grade for his environmental policies.[7] The same is true of many other recent environmental histories. These studies discuss the rich environmental history of Lincoln's lifetime and identify key environmental events, such as the passage of the Yosemite Valley Grant Act, without offering judgments or ranking Lincoln's environmental achievements against those of other U.S. presidents.

Lincoln's personal relationship with the natural environment and his political policies concerning the environment are perhaps too complicated to render a ranking or a grade. No attempt to grade or rank Lincoln is made in this study, nor does this study advance the argument that Lincoln was a "green" president whose political agenda specifically included measures to improve America's natural environment. As Graham suggests, not until the late nineteenth century did U.S. presidents begin to articulate and advance environmental agendas. But Lincoln lived through a critical period in

U.S. environmental history. In both his personal and political life, he dealt with environmental issues and learned to adapt to the environmental changes taking place in his nation. His relationship to the natural environment, both direct and indirect, was lifelong, and it was still evolving when his life abruptly ended at the beginning of his second presidential term. Lincoln left for us an environmental biography worthy of study.

I WAS RAISED TO FARM WORK

"I was raised to farm work, which I continued till I was twenty-two," Abraham Lincoln wrote in an autobiographical letter to fellow attorney Jesse W. Fell in 1859.[1] Lincoln's environmental biography begins on farms in the American Midwest. When Lincoln was born shortly after the turn of the nineteenth century, about 90 percent of Americans lived on farms.[2] Lincoln's American ancestors were farmers who, in search of open land and fertile soil to farm, migrated southward and westward from New England, where Lincolns from Great Britain originally settled in the mid-seventeenth century, to New Jersey, to Pennsylvania, to Virginia, to the Carolinas, to Kentucky, where Abraham Lincoln was born in 1809, and then to Indiana and Illinois. Lincoln's mother's American ancestors, the Hanks family, made a similar generational journey.[3] All of Lincoln's presidential predecessors were also born on farms or plantations. But unlike, for example, Thomas Jefferson and Andrew Jackson, the Lincolns who eventually migrated to the American Midwest were neither gentlemen farmers nor plantation owners.

Environmental historians suggest that many early American settlers might have viewed this "new" continent in biblical terms, as a potential new Garden of Eden, a land of plenty and a chance for humankind to create in this seemingly lush and boundless American landscape an earthly utopia.[4] The first writers from Great Britain and Europe to describe the American natural landscape, such as John

Smith, Robert Beverley, and Michel-Guillaume Jean de Crèvecoeur, articulated this view, depicting North America as a land of plenty waiting to be populated by ambitious settlers—an environmental utopia with fertile soil to be farmed, bays and rivers teeming with fish, and an endless supply of timber from dense forests. But for most American farmers of the early nineteenth century, including the Lincolns, carving a living from the rugged American wilderness was hard work. Basic survival was difficult enough; prosperity was merely a utopian dream.

The Lincolns were classic subsistence pioneer farmers; they farmed to survive. They tended some livestock to provide milk and meat, and they raised wheat, potatoes, corn, pumpkins, and other crops to put on their tables to nourish the family; perhaps some leftover wheat or corn might be busheled and sold during years of bounteous harvests. They did odd jobs such as carpentry to earn money to purchase products that they could not make by hand. They hunted wild animals and fished to supplement their vegetable and grain diets. They owned no slaves to assist with the farm work. These early nineteenth-century subsistence farmers lived in no rural American Garden of Eden. The process of setting up and maintaining a productive farm was laborious. Subsistence farmers like the Lincolns cleared woodlands with axes, uprooted stumps with shovels and picks, created fields for crops with homemade plows, split trees to make fence posts and rails. When the soil became depleted in one field after several growing seasons, farmers cleared another field and then another. Most subsistence farmers lived in crude shacks and small cabins that they built themselves from materials hacked out of the wilderness, and they constructed their own furniture. The Kentucky cabin in which Lincoln was born had a dirt floor. When the Lincolns relocated from Kentucky to Indiana in 1816, when Abraham was seven years old, they lived for several months in a three-sided lean-to.[5] Describing his family's move to Indiana in a short autobiographical sketch written, in third person, for the 1860 presidential campaign, Lincoln stated that his father, Thomas Lincoln, settled "in an unbroken forest; and the clearing away of surplus wood was the great task a head." Abe, "though very young, was large of his age and had an axe put into his hands at once; and from that till within his twentythird year, he was almost constantly handling that most useful instrument—less, of course, in plowing and harvesting seasons."[6]

Lincoln did not speak or write a great deal about his early years on family farms, perhaps because he came to be embarrassed by that segment of his life or because such a life lacked any distinctive or noteworthy elements. In 1860, when asked by the journalist John L. Scripps to describe his youth and young adulthood for a biographical sketch for the forthcoming presidential campaign, Lincoln was evasive. Scripps later wrote to William Herndon, Lincoln's law partner, who was composing a biography of Lincoln shortly after Lincoln's death, about his campaign interview with Lincoln: "The chief difficulty I had to encounter, was to induce him to communicate the homely facts and incidents of his early life. He seemed to be painfully impressed with the extreme poverty of his early surroundings—the utter absence of all romantic and heroic elements." Lincoln emphatically dismissed the importance of that period of his life: "Why Scripps, it is a great piece of folly to attempt to make anything out of me or my early life. It can all be condensed in to a single sentence, and that sentence you will find in Gray's Elegy: 'The short and simple annals of the poor.' That's my life, and that's all that you or anyone else can make of it."[7] Lincoln once referred to his life on the Kentucky farm where he was born as "stinted living."[8] This comment provides testimony to the material hardship that marked Lincoln's early years on farms. The Lincoln family, like many other subsistence pioneer farmers, often experienced food shortages; many Lincoln family meals consisted solely of potatoes grown on the farm.[9]

To be a subsistence farmer in the United States in the early nineteenth century was to live close to the environment—and to be at its mercy, to engage in a daily struggle with the forces of nature for mere survival. Land had to be cleared of trees, brush, and thickets; crops and livestock had to be protected from foraging wild animals. A random act of nature over which farmers had no control and for which they had virtually no defense, such as drought or a deluge, an early or late frost, or a botanical disease, could ruin a season's crops and plunge a frontier farm family into starvation.[10] A series of volcanic eruptions in Indonesia between 1811 and 1818, the period of Lincoln's childhood, caused cold weather and crop failures around the globe, even as far away as the United States.[11] Diseases and illnesses of all kinds spread through farming communities, and medical help for the sick was often unavailable. As a young child, Lincoln learned a poignant lesson about the power that nature held over his life and fate. When his family was still living in Knob Creek, Kentucky, young Abraham and family members spent a Saturday planting corn and pumpkin seeds in a large seven-acre field. "The next Sunday morning there came a big rain in the hills. It did not rain a drop in the valley," recollected Lincoln many years later, "but the water coming down through the gorges washed ground, corn, pumpkin seeds and all clear off the field."[12] An environmental event over which he had no control, a thunderstorm in the hills, destroyed his family's crops in the valley.

Young Abraham learned a more profound and emotionally painful lesson about nature's power over his life two years after the Lincoln family relocated from Kentucky to Little Pigeon Creek, Indiana (a move, Lincoln later explained, necessitated by land title problems in Kentucky). In the autumn of 1818, when Lincoln was nine years old, milk sickness swept through this rural Indiana community. Milk sickness came from cow's milk. In the American Midwest, especially in wooded areas, the white snakeroot plant grew in the wild. Cows would often ingest the plant as they grazed. Their milk became poisonous, but farmers often did not recognize symptoms of the illness in the cows. People who drank this poisoned milk often became grievously sick; they grew weak, their skin became pale, they began retching and vomiting, and they developed a high fever. Some survived the sickness, but often the ill individuals, pioneer farmers who could not easily receive medical attention, fell into a coma and died. Thousands of midwesterners died of milk sickness during the nineteenth century; the illness became as feared as killer diseases such as cholera and smallpox. Lincoln's mother, Nancy, and his great-aunt and uncle, Thomas and Elizabeth Sparrow, contracted milk sickness in the outbreak that swept through their rural community in 1818. All three died of the illness. Young Abe helped his father build his mother's coffin.[13]

Biographers have identified a melancholy streak in Lincoln's personality. He reportedly suffered throughout his life from bouts of depression, and according to some of his friends, he even demonstrated suicidal tendencies. He refused to carry on his person a pocketknife for fear that he might intentionally injure himself with the weapon. The death of his mother, when Abraham was at such a young age, could have contributed to his lifelong battles with depression.[14] Death was certainly a frequent visitor to frontier families. In Lincoln's time, one-fourth of all American children lost a parent before they reached the age of fifteen.[15] A year after Nancy Lincoln's death, Abraham's father, Thomas, brought a mother's love and care to his motherless children by marrying Sarah Bush Johnson, a widow with three children. Abraham's stepmother became to him a kind and loving mother. Nonetheless, the death of his mother, and the cruel manner of her death, undoubtedly shocked nine-year-old Abraham.

Moreover, the death of Nancy Lincoln might have hammered home to young Abraham a troubling environmental lesson: nature can be cruel, even deadly poisonous. His mother died from drinking fresh cow's milk, a beverage traditionally associated with good health, not sickness. The cow had passed the illness to Lincoln's mother through the simple and natural act of grazing in a wooded field where poisonous plants randomly grew. To be so directly dependent on the natural environment for one's needs, as the Lincoln family was, made life full of risk and left them dangerously vulnerable. The episode in Kentucky with the washed-away corn and pumpkin seeds conveyed to young Abraham the lesson that an act of nature can negate a hard day's work. The death of his mother brought notice that living so close to and so immediately dependent on the natural environment could be deadly.

Lincoln lived on family farms until he was twenty-two years old. Biographers agree that Lincoln, as he approached manhood, sought to escape the subsistence farming that his family practiced.[16] Although he worked hard to help sustain his family as a child and young man, becoming particularly efficient at wielding an ax to chop wood and split rails, Lincoln began to resent the arduous physical labor that a farming life required. He later claimed that he came to understand the horrible lives of slaves because his father treated him like one on the family farm.[17] Abe was plowing fields by age seven.[18] Often Thomas Lincoln would hire out his strong and healthy son Abraham to neighboring farms to assist with the chores, and the father kept the wages that his son earned, which Thomas Lincoln was legally entitled to do until his son reached the age of twenty-one. Abraham might have come to see agricultural labor in biblical terms—his biological mother, who was at least semiliterate, owned a Bible and read it to young Abe—but farms to him, and to most subsistence farmers, were not Gardens of Eden.[19] In the book of Genesis, after Adam and Eve commit sin, God condemns them to a life of arduous labor: "in the sweat of thy face shalt thou eat bread, till thou return unto the ground."[20] Many years after he left the family farm, in a lecture on new discoveries and inventions, Lincoln alluded to that passage from Genesis, stating that "in consequence of the first transgression, *labor* was imposed on the race, as a *penalty*—a *curse*" that forced a human being to become "a tiller of the ground."[21] By the time he was a teenager, Lincoln sought a way to escape the laborious subsistence farming that had occupied generations of American Lincolns; he did not wish to become a tiller of the ground. Escape from physical labor would not be easy, however. Lincoln entered adulthood during a time when only about 5 percent of American men made their living in an occupation that did not require manual labor.[22]

Other elements of the farming life and environment, besides the backbreaking labor, did not suit Lincoln. He had attended what he later called "A.B.C. schools" for several months during his boyhood,[23] and he had learned to read. His stepmother managed to bring some books into the home; he was able to borrow others. As a child, Lincoln read as frequently as he could; he loved books such as *Aesop's Fables*, Mason Locke Weems's *The Life of George Washington*, John Bunyan's *Pilgrim's Progress*, and Daniel Defoe's *Robinson Crusoe*. Occasionally, Lincoln read rather than performing his farm chores and was sometimes cuffed by his virtually illiterate father for this habit.[24] Lincoln's rural environment offered little in the way of books or education. When he reached his teenage years, however, Lincoln began to imagine a life off the farm and perhaps an occupation that

As a child and young adult, Abraham Lincoln labored in midwestern cornfields like the one captured in this early twentieth-century photo. Library of Congress.

revolved around books rather than the field, the ax, and the plow. Out of curiosity, Lincoln, as a teenager, began to sit in on trials when the circuit court made its way into his area. Perhaps these experiences awakened the possibility of the law as a future occupation.[25] Lincoln certainly did not want to become a subsistence farmer like his father, a career that provided so little intellectual stimulation and offered such minimal opportunity for upward social and financial mobility. A subsistence farmer's main ambition was to make the next harvest, to avoid starvation. Lincoln had developed ambitions beyond subsistence farming.

Rural living in Lincoln's time was often isolating. If there were no nearby town, farmers worked and lived mainly in isolation. They dwelled far from neighbors and had few opportunities to gather and meet. Perhaps a minister might occasionally pass through and offer Sunday services to local farmers. Perhaps farmers met at a local store or at a gristmill where their wheat or corn was processed. But there were few community gathering places where a bright young man like Lincoln could regularly meet with peers to discuss their lives and the issues of the day. He never took to hunting, an outdoor activity that might have connected him to other boys and young men living on Indiana farms. He once shot a wild turkey, regretted it, and never killed another wild animal. Midwestern winters were particularly isolating for farm families. Blizzards would make the crude rural roads virtually impassable for weeks. At such times, farm families would be confined to their homes, separated from neighbors and community, virtually imprisoned by their harsh natural environment. When he reached his teens, Lincoln began to imagine living in a different kind of environment from the one in which he was raised. His imagination might have been stimulated by two riverboat trips that he took during his young adulthood.

In April 1828, when Lincoln was nineteen years old, he and a friend, Allen Gentry, were hired to take a flatboat load of farm produce down the Mississippi River for sale in New Orleans. He would make another such trip three years later. The New Orleans excursions were eye-opening for young Lincoln. For the first time, he experienced an urban community and way of life. By the 1820s, New Orleans was already becoming a bustling metropolitan port city with stores, hotels, churches, theaters, dance halls, and eateries. Occupations other than those present in a farming community were on display in New Orleans.[26] Moreover, by this time, steamboats were traversing the Mississippi River, vividly illustrating the power of the steam engine. A steamboat could journey upriver against the current, revealing to young Lincoln that the forces and rhythms of nature, like a downstream current, could be conquered by a man-made mechanism. Lincoln's payment for the flatboat excursion downriver in 1828 included return passage aboard a steamboat.[27] In his 1883 memoir, *Life on the Mississippi*, Mark Twain described the Mississippi River journey for upriver tradesmen before the arrival of the steamboat: "They [the keelboats] floated and sailed from the upper rivers to New Orleans, changed cargoes there, and were tediously warped and poled back by hand. A voyage down and back sometimes occupied nine months." But according to Twain, "By and by the steamboat intruded," and then upstream traders could still run their keelboats or flatboats downstream but return as deck passengers on the steamers, reducing the round-trip journey by months.[28]

In March 1830, when Lincoln was twenty-one years old, his family moved again, this time from Indiana to Illinois. The move involved an arduous two-week, 225-mile trek through the wilderness, with the family's belongings packed into wagons drawn by oxen and horses. The Lincolns settled in Macon County, near the town of Decatur and the Sangamon River.[29] Abraham helped his family build a dwelling and cut a new farm out of the rugged Illinois wilderness. He brought in extra income by splitting rails, a task at which he excelled. By now, however, Lincoln's legal and financial obligations to his family had ended; he had reached the age of twenty-one and would be able to keep any wages that he earned rather than turn his pay over to his father. He was also free to leave the family and strike out on his own. But Lincoln remained on the family farm through the harvest season of 1830. It would be his last year as a farmer.

Perhaps an act of nature, an environmental catastrophe for some farmers who lived in his community, prompted Lincoln to finally leave the Illinois family farm for good. The winter of 1830–31 became known in Illinois as the Winter of the Deep Snow. It began with a three-foot snowfall between Christmas and New Year's Day. During the next several weeks, nineteen separate snowstorms hit the area. For weeks straight, evening temperatures dropped below zero degrees. Livestock froze to death. The Lincolns and other subsistence farmers faced serious food shortages. Most of the region's farmers were housebound, unable to trek through the snowdrifts to visit neighbors. In February, Lincoln, traveling to a rail-splitting job a couple of miles from his family's home, broke through some ice and got his feet wet, which resulted in a severe case of frostbite that kept him housebound for a month.[30] Bad weather, according to one Lincoln scholar who has studied his psychological state, often triggered Lincoln's bouts of melancholy,[31] so this winter on the farm must have been particularly trying for him. Again, he undoubtedly realized that the natural environment had a firm grasp on his life and fate, but that spring, an escape plan would present itself.

In the spring of 1831, the Lincoln family made another move—to Coles County, Illinois. Lincoln also made his second flatboat excursion to New Orleans, again transporting Illinois farm products to the city's urban population, on behalf of a merchant, Denton Offutt. When he returned to Illinois in the early summer, Lincoln opted not to go back to the family farm in Coles County; he settled instead in the village of New Salem, a town on the Sangamon River in Sangamon County, where Offutt had opened a store and recruited Lincoln to be his clerk. For a time, Lincoln continued to supplement his clerk's income by hiring himself out to split rails and perform other tasks that he had performed on his family's farms. But Lincoln's life as a farmer was over; he would never again reside on a farm. As one Lincoln scholar put it, "The forced marriage between Lincoln and agricultural work was dissolved as soon as the young man was in a position to do so."[32] Lincoln's departure from the family farm was an act of personal emancipation—he had come to see his life of hard labor on the family farm under his father's rule as a kind of enslavement.[33] At age twenty-two, when Lincoln arrived in New Salem, he had a new occupation and new identity—store clerk—that disconnected him from the farming environment of his youth and young adulthood.

New Salem, Illinois, was not a thriving metropolis during the 1830s when Lincoln arrived there. It was, as one Lincoln scholar described it, "a one-road village cut from the forest."[34] But it contained a tavern, a mill where local farmers brought their grain for processing, a blacksmith shop, Offutt's store, and a few other shops where the surrounding community of farmers conducted their business.[35] Newspapers, largely absent in the farming communities where Lincoln had previously lived, were available for purchase in New Salem. Moreover, New Salem offered a debating club and literary society that Lincoln eagerly joined. It provided him a venue for discussing books and issues of the day that were not farm-related, as well as the opportunity to develop his public-speaking and argumentation skills. Members of the club debated weighty topics of the day, such as slavery and women's rights, which sparked Lincoln's interest in politics.[36]

Lincoln quickly became active and well known in the small community of New Salem. Significantly, the first major community project to which Lincoln devoted considerable time and effort concerned the local natural environment. New Salem could thrive as rural town only if it could serve as a trading post for farmers and merchants who wanted to transport their goods downriver for sale. The Sangamon River, however, was a meandering waterway too shallow and narrow in some places to accommodate larger vessels. Shortly after moving to New Salem, Lincoln joined a group of local men who conceived the idea of "straightening" the Sangamon River by digging new channels. The new channels would reduce the distance between two points on the river and also widen and deepen the river, which would enable larger craft, like small steamboats, to travel downriver without getting tangled in streamside obstacles or bottoming out in shallow water. These boats could then transport New Salem's agricultural products up and down the Sangamon River for sale. Lincoln, having spent the first twenty-two years of his life very much dependent on and even controlled by the natural environment, was now involved in a community project that would attempt to reshape the natural environment to accommodate the local population's economic needs. The project to reshape the Sangamon River was ultimately unsuccessful, but it played a key role in the commencement of Lincoln's political career.[37]

In March 1832, less than a year after he moved to New Salem, Lincoln sent a long statement to the local newspaper, *Sangamo Journal*, announcing his intention to run for a seat in the Illinois state assembly, his first written and published political document. Significantly, the main theme of the statement—the key issue on which he would base his candidacy—was "internal improvements" that would facilitate the shipping of products over long distances. "Time and experience have verified to a demonstration, the public utility of internal improvements," Lincoln stated after announcing his candidacy in his first paragraph. "That the poorest and most thinly populated countries would be greatly benefitted by the opening of good roads, and in the clearing of navigable streams within their limits, is what no person will deny." Then, perhaps reflecting on the recent unsuccessful effort to alter the course of the Sangamon River, he added, "But yet it is folly to undertake works of this or any other kind, without first knowing that we are able to finish them—as half finished work generally proves to be labor lost." He continued his discussion of the river, stating that with its drifting timber and meandering channels, "it never can be practically useful to any great extent, without being greatly improved by art"—a creative reshaping of the river. Lincoln went on to say that securing funding to improve the river would get his full support if he were elected.[38]

The next month, April 1832, Lincoln enlisted in the local militia and left New Salem to participate in the Black Hawk War. He remained in service until July, then returned to New Salem to engage in campaigning until Election Day, August 6. Although Lincoln received the great majority of votes cast in New Salem, where he had already become very popular, he did not win enough votes in the rest of Sangamon County to secure a seat in the Illinois assembly. Nonetheless, during this first political campaign, Lincoln had found a key issue that would drive his early political career: government funding for internal improvements such as canals, railroads, roads, bridges, and harbor upgrades to facilitate transportation and trade.

Lincoln remained in New Salem for six years. Besides operating Offutt's store, he supplemented his living by doing farm chores. Eventually, Offutt's store failed. Lincoln and a partner opened a store, but it also failed a short time later. In 1834, however, Lincoln had been appointed postmaster, and he had essentially taught himself, from books on the subject, land surveying to supplement his postmaster's income. At this time, surveying offered a potentially good living, as qualified surveyors were in great demand in a locality that was experiencing waves of new settlers wanting to purchase tracts of land and establish farms. But like farming, surveying often required battling nature and the natural environment, traipsing through woods, fields, and swamps to take measurements and record data. Lincoln's reading, however, was pointing him in another, more appealing occupational direction: the law.

Living in New Salem, off the family farm and away from its grinding daily chores, Lincoln could devote more time to reading. His debating and literary club passed books around, and Lincoln read widely for pleasure. He developed a lifelong love for the plays of William Shakespeare and the poetry of Lord George Gordon Byron and Robert Burns. But he also viewed literacy as a means to personal and professional advancement. He began reading, at this time in his life, books that might help him improve his position in the world. He studied grammar texts with the idea of improving his writing. He read books on science. He also commenced an informal study of law by tackling William Blackstone's *Commentaries on the Laws of England*, first published in the 1760s, which had become a required text for anyone aspiring to become an attorney in the United States during the nineteenth century. Lincoln had met several lawyers during his short service in the Black Hawk War, and they encouraged him to consider the legal profession.[39]

In Lincoln's time, becoming a lawyer did not require earning a college degree and then attending law school. Although many lawyers of the time had attended colleges or universities, many also entered the legal profession after a period of informal study and apprenticeship. Academic degrees were not required to take the state bar exam in Illinois. Lincoln's study of the law was informal. He read the key legal texts and did some informal paralegal work while living in New Salem. Being literate, Lincoln often crafted real estate contracts and other legal documents for illiterate or barely literate local farmers.[40] In 1834, Lincoln again ran for a seat in the Illinois assembly, and this time he was elected. He was reelected two years later. During legislative sessions, Lincoln began working with other assemblymen to draft legislation. He was becoming a good legal writer. When the legislature was not in session, Lincoln returned to New Salem and began work with a noted local attorney, Bowling Green. In September 1836, the Illinois Supreme Court examined Lincoln and certified his qualifications to practice law. He received his law license on September 9, 1836, and was formally admitted to the Illinois Bar on March 1, 1837.

During the six years that Lincoln lived in New Salem, the town had undergone a serious decline in population. The dream of making New Salem an important Mississippi River port had failed. The town could not support a store like the one Offutt and later Lincoln operated. In May 1836, New Salem's post office closed. By this time, however, Lincoln had begun to outgrow New Salem. He was earning money as a land surveyor, but his study of law was opening professional opportunities beyond those available in a dying frontier town. In April 1837, a month after he had been admitted to the Illinois Bar, Lincoln moved to Springfield, Illinois.

Springfield, which would become the capital of Illinois in 1839, was, when Lincoln arrived, a much larger and more cosmopolitan town than New Salem. Its population was fifteen hundred. Its streets were unpaved, but the town held both wooden and brick buildings, a county courthouse, several churches, hotels, stores, and doctors' and lawyers' offices.[41] The town had its own newspapers, the *Springfield Illinois Republican*, *Sangamo Journal*, and *Springfield Morning Courier*. It also boasted a Young Men's Lyceum, a public forum offering young men the opportunity to speak on the important political and social issues of the day. In Springfield, Lincoln began his career as an attorney. He became a law partner to John Todd Stuart, and the two men developed a thriving law practice that included both civil and criminal cases. Lincoln had won reelection to the Illinois legislature in 1836, and he worked with several other assemblymen to move the state's capital from Vandalia to Springfield.

Lincoln's divorce from rural America and from farming as a means of livelihood was now complete. He had found an occupation based on books and legal documents, not the ax and plow or a riverboat or a land surveyor's tool kit. His work would be completed in law offices and courtrooms, not in the rugged natural environment, and he would no longer be as vulnerable to the forces of nature that had so dominated his boyhood and young adulthood. Several years after settling in Springfield, Lincoln sent a letter to his friend Joshua F. Speed. Speed had asked Lincoln a question about farming, and Lincoln replied, "As to your farm matter, I have no sympathy with you.

I have no farm, nor ever expect to have; and, consequently, have not studied the subject enough to be much interested with it."[42] Lincoln was now an attorney and a politician, not a farmer. He served in the Illinois assembly until 1842 and was elected to the U.S. House of Representatives in 1846.

Lincoln's move from the farm was more than a change in occupation; it marked a change in his identity. As one Lincoln scholar put it, "He tore himself away from a confined life."[43] Lincoln was finished with the arduous labor and the confining lifestyle of a farm. His new occupation promised upward social and financial mobility; it allowed him to work with his brain, not his body. It also insulated him, in many ways, from the harsh and unforgiving rural environment in which he had grown up, an environment that had provided a "stinted living" and that had taken his mother from him at a young age. Significantly, as his biographers have pointed out, Lincoln, after he became an attorney and moved to Springfield, distanced himself from his father, who for Abraham personified the limiting farming life from which he had walked away. He seldom visited his parents. When Lincoln married Mary Todd in 1842, after an on-and-off engagement, he did not invite his parents to attend the wedding. The Lincolns named their fourth son after Thomas Lincoln, but they called the boy Tad rather than Thomas or Tom.[44]

In late May 1849, shortly after Lincoln completed his single term in Congress, he received letters from his stepbrother, John D. Johnston, and other family members about a serious illness that had inflicted Thomas Lincoln. In his letter, Johnston wrote that Lincoln's father is "yet a Live & that is all & he Craves to See you all the time & he wants you to Come—if you ar able to git hure, for you are his only Child that is of his own flush & blood & it is nothing more than natere for him to crave to see you." Augustus H. Chapman, another relation, also told Lincoln, "He is very anxious to see you before he dies & I am told that His cries for you for the last few days are truly Heart Rendering." Lincoln did visit his father in Illinois at the end of May when he returned from his congressional duties in Washington.[45] Thomas Lincoln recovered from that illness, but eighteen months later, when Thomas was again seriously ill and family members summoned Abraham to his father's sickbed, Abraham balked. On January 12, 1851, he wrote a terse letter to his stepbrother stating that he would not be visiting his father this time, even though he was living only about a hundred miles away. Mary Lincoln was ill, and Abraham explained to his stepbrother that he would not leave his wife during her illness. Lincoln advised his stepbrother to encourage his father "to remember to call upon, and confide in, our great, and good, and merciful Maker; who will not turn away from him in any extremity." Lincoln continued with another sentence in this vein, then added, "Say to him that if we could meet now, it is doubtful whether it would not be more painful than pleasant."[46] Thomas Lincoln died five days after his son wrote that letter.

Not until ten years later did Lincoln visit his father's gravesite. In his 1888 biography of Lincoln, William H. Herndon, Lincoln's Springfield law partner, wrote that in February 1861, before leaving Illinois to travel to Washington, D.C., to become president, Lincoln performed "one more duty—an act of filial devotion." He rode to Coles County and visited his aging stepmother and "the grave of his father, old Thomas Lincoln, which had been unmarked and neglected for almost a decade, and left directions that a suitable stone should be placed there to mark the spot."[47] As a young man, Lincoln had divorced himself from his father's life, a life closely connected to the natural environment.

By the time of Thomas Lincoln's death, Abraham and Mary Lincoln were living comfortably in Springfield. They had three sons and were residing in a spacious and fashionably appointed home. The Lincolns' Springfield home symbolized Abraham's transformation from a frontier farmer and store clerk into a successful attorney. The house was a one-and-a-half-story cottage when the Lincolns purchased and occupied it in 1844, but it was remodeled and expanded over the next several years into a two-story, ten-room dwelling in the fashionable Greek Revival style of the day. The formal parlor and other rooms held stylish rococo furnishings.[48]

Abraham Lincoln, who was born in a log cabin in rural Kentucky, purchased this fashionable Victorian home in Springfield, Illinois, in 1844.
Library of Congress.

By the time the Lincolns had purchased their Springfield home,
Abraham was already a very successful lawyer and a well-known
Illinois politician whose main political issue was the one that had
driven his first political campaign: internal improvements. This effort to bend and shape the natural environment, which he had first
embraced shortly after leaving his family's farm and settling in New
Salem, occupied Lincoln for the rest of his political career.

INTERNAL IMPROVEMENTS

Thomas Jefferson, in his *Notes on the State of Virginia*, published in 1787, envisioned the newly formed United States of America as a nation of yeoman farmers who would make their living tilling the soil. Small, independent farmers, like the ancestors of Abraham Lincoln, who first settled along the East Coast during the seventeenth century and whose descendants migrated westward across the continent in search of open spaces to establish homesteads and fertile lands to farm, were, in Jefferson's mind, the exemplars of American democracy. These landowning American farmers would remain fiercely independent, free from oppression by overlords or bosses, and this independent citizenry would become and forever remain the cornerstone of a democratic nation. "Those who labor in the earth are the chosen people of God," Jefferson wrote.[1] In Jefferson's view, the United States would remain a nation of farmers for centuries to come. The new nation's seemingly endless unsettled spaces and rich soil would enable Jefferson's American dream. But even as Jefferson was writing those words, as thousands of farmers like the Lincolns were migrating westward, seeking new lands to farm, the new nation was beginning to undergo significant economic, social, and cultural changes; it was beginning to pull slowly away from its agricultural roots, and this transition would have lasting impacts on the American landscape and natural environment.

Shortly after George Washington became the new nation's first president in 1789, he commissioned his secretary of the treasury,

Alexander Hamilton, to compose a report on American manufacturing, which was still in its infancy in this new nation of farmers but which Washington believed merited serious study and analysis. Secretary Hamilton, working with coauthor Tench Coxe, a Pennsylvanian who had served as a member of the Articles of Confederation Congress, authored a document titled *Report on the Subject of Manufactures*, which they delivered to President Washington and the U.S. Congress in 1791. "The expediency of encouraging manufactures in the United States, which was no long since deemed very questionable, appears to be pretty generally admitted," stated the introduction to Hamilton and Coxe's report. The report went on to state, "It has been maintained that agriculture is, not only, the most productive but the only productive species of industry. The reality of this suggestion, in either respect, has, however, not been verified by any accurate detail of facts and calculations; and the general arguments, which are adduced to prove it, are rather subtil and paradoxical, than solid or convincing." The report offered some concrete suggestions to spur American manufacturing, including government subsidies to new industries; government support for internal improvements such as roads, canals, and bridges to facilitate trade across the nation; and a high tariff on imported manufactured goods to encourage Americans to produce and purchase manufactured products made in the United States.[2] Hamilton and Coxe's report forecast some of the key positions that Abraham Lincoln would later embrace when he began his political career as a member of the Whig Party during the 1830s.

There was a good deal of governmental opposition to the *Report on the Subject of Manufactures.* President Washington's secretary of state, Thomas Jefferson, was, unsurprisingly, sharply critical of the report's findings and recommendations. He contended that developing manufacturing in the United States might threaten his notion of a nation composed mainly of independent farmers. Americans who worked for manufacturers, rather than for themselves on their own land, could lose the independent spirit that Jefferson viewed as the key element of a democratic government. In actuality, however, by the time Hamilton and Coxe's report appeared, manufacturing had already established a toehold in the new nation. An iron smelting factory had opened in New England in 1643,[3] almost a century and a half before Hamilton and Coxe filed their report. By 1700, there were ninety sawmills in New England.[4] Gilbert Stuart, the great eighteenth-century portrait painter, was born in 1755 in a snuff mill on a stream in Saunderstown, Rhode Island, that also supported a nearby gristmill. By the middle of the eighteenth century, scores of gristmills, for grinding corn, and snuff mills, for grinding tobacco, were operating in the American colonies, run mainly by water power. Small factories sprouted across the colonies, producing nails, tools, pots and pans, and other metal products that farmers like the Lincolns used in their daily lives.

In the 1770s, thirty years before Lincoln's birth, steam engines had begun to appear in Great Britain. These basic machines used steam to propel pistons to create what is now known as horsepower. Over the next few decades, a factory system developed in Great Britain. By the thousands, Britons left farm communities and settled in factory towns. Many of the first factories used steam engines to produce textiles, spinning raw cotton into cloth to be used in clothing and household products. In 1790, Samuel Slater, an Englishman who had migrated to America the year before at age twenty-one, established a spinning mill on the Blackstone River in Pawtucket, Rhode Island. Having worked in British factories from boyhood, Slater was able to copy the British machine designs for use in his Rhode Island mill, and he upgraded his mill with more powerful machinery three years later. Slater, sometimes called the "Father of the Industrial Revolution," established what became, over the next several decades, a thriving New England textile business. Textile mills sprouted up all over New England—in Lowell and Chicopee, Massachusetts; in Dover, Manchester, and Nashua, New Hampshire; in Maine along the Penobscot River—turning Southern-grown cotton into textile products for sale to American consumers. By 1829, as Lincoln was reaching adulthood on his family farm, imagining a life different from farming, a factory system like the one in Great Britain was in place in New England. In 1833, in Lowell, Massachusetts, alone, there were eight textile mills that employed five thousand workers.[5] Significantly, "technology" became an English word in 1829.[6]

The same basic steam engine used in textile mills would revolutionize transportation. Before the steam engine, land vehicles ran mainly by animal power, and vessels moved across the waters with the current or the wind or by the power of men wielding oars or paddles. But in the early nineteenth century, the steam engine was adapted for use on boats. Robert Fulton, a Pennsylvania farmer and artist born in 1765, relocated as a young man to England and then to Paris at a time when industrialization was taking hold in Europe. Fulton began using his artistic skills to imagine and design new machines. He patented a machine that dredged rivers and began experimenting with a steam-powered boat. Fulton returned to the United States in 1806 and built *Clermont*, a steamboat that made its debut on the Hudson River in 1807, two years before Lincoln was born. In its maiden voyage, *Clermont* left a dock in New York City and traveled 150 miles upstream to Albany in thirty-two hours.[7] By 1828, when Abraham Lincoln made his first flatboat journey on the Mississippi River, steamboats were operating on the Mississippi and many major American rivers.

Even Lincoln's original profession, farming, was being transformed by new machines. In 1793, Eli Whitney, a Massachusetts native born in 1765 and living in Georgia, invented a machine to separate cotton seeds from cotton fiber. Before the invention of Whitney's cotton gin, this task was laboriously performed by hand, at the rate of about five pounds of cotton per day. The gin could process ten times that amount. Whitney's invention allowed cotton to become a cash crop in the American South, which increased the economic value of the region's slaves. Southern cotton was shipped to New England and Great Britain for processing in textile mills.

Two additional farming inventions, which could have enhanced Lincoln's life had he remained a farmer, appeared during the 1830s. In 1834, Cyrus McCormick, a Virginian born in 1809, the same year as Lincoln, received a patent for a mechanical reaper, a horse-drawn device that cut and gathered wheat, a task that had previously been done by farmers like the Lincolns by hand and scythe. Two years later, John Deere, who was born in Vermont in 1804, moved to Illinois, while Lincoln was serving in the state legislature, and opened a machine shop in Grand Detour that produced hand tools for local farmers. A year later, he invented and began to produce a plow with a steel blade. Earlier plows had blades made of either wood or iron, which the soil stuck to during plowing. Deere's more durable steel plow cut more smoothly through the soil, greatly reducing the time and effort it took for a farmer to plow a field. Lincoln's contemporaries were transforming American agriculture, bringing to it the manufactured products of the Industrial Revolution.

The most prominent symbol of the new American industrial and commercial order appeared in 1826: the locomotive. That year, a locomotive powered by a steam engine was tested in Hoboken, New Jersey. This first American locomotive could maintain a steady speed of twelve miles per hour.[8] Within fifteen years, locomotive-powered trains, moving much faster than the one that debuted in Hoboken, were crisscrossing the United States. In 1830, the entire country had only seventy-three miles of railroad tracks. By 1840, more than three thousand miles of tracks had been laid, and ten years later, almost nine thousand miles of railroad tracks connected the settled regions of the United States in a growing transportation network.[9] The locomotive transformed the nation. Before the invention of the locomotive, Americans journeyed around the country mainly on horseback, in horse-drawn vehicles such as wagons and stagecoaches, or on waterways. Mail and products were transported the same way. Now a train could cover the distance between major cities such as New York and Boston or Philadelphia or Washington, D.C., in less than a day. The East Coast and Lincoln's Midwest were soon connected by railroads. When Lincoln began his term in the U.S. House of Representatives in 1847, he was able to travel from Illinois to Washington by train. The first locomotives to appear in the United States were British imports, but by 1840, locomotive factories were operating in the United States, employing American workers in the nation's developing industrial economy.

Besides providing transportation for Americans eager to visit relatives across the country or travel to places that they had read about but had never hoped to see, the railroad facilitated trade, agricultural expansion across the nation, and manufacturing. The products

The locomotive became the prime symbol of the Industrial Revolution. Abraham Lincoln strongly endorsed railroad construction and served as an attorney for railroad companies. Library of Congress.

manufactured in New England's textile mills could be efficiently shipped and sold across the country. Deere's steel plows, manufactured in Illinois, could be shipped by rail to Northeastern and Southern farmers. Farm products—cotton, sugar, and tobacco from the South, corn and wheat grown in the Midwest—could be packed into train cars and transported for sale in urban areas where residents did not grow their own produce. The ability to move products around the nation efficiently, Lincoln later stated in one of his 1858 debates with Stephen Douglas, "produces commerce, brings us together, and makes us better friends. We like one another the more for it." Lincoln believed that trade "accommodations are the cements which bind together the different parts of this Union—that instead of being a thing to 'divide the house'—figuratively expressing the Union,—they tend to sustain it; they are the props of the house tending always to hold it up."[10]

The railroad and the steamboat were, in a sense, altering the natural landscape, or at least Americans' conception of it, by reducing travel time between two points on a map. After the invention of the steamboat, a rushing river current no longer made an upriver journey as formidable or prohibitive, as Lincoln discovered on his journeys to and from New Orleans; a machine-driven boat could push against the current. Railroads rapidly cut through areas where no natural or man-made highways existed, and they crossed rivers and deep canyons over bridges, enabling travel between two locations separated by natural obstacles—forests, hills, valleys, and rivers. As railroads were expanding during the 1830s and 1840s, another invention, the electrical telegraph, was also shrinking the country, enabling messages to be sent almost instantly between two distant locations.

The journey that Abraham Lincoln made in his early adulthood, away from the farm, its economy, and its natural and social environment, was the same one that the nation was making during the same time period. For the remainder of the nineteenth century, farming would remain a vital economic element in the United States, especially in the South and the West. But the Industrial Revolution, a term coined in France in 1810, the year after Lincoln's birth,[11] was occurring in the United States during Lincoln's lifetime, and as a young man, Lincoln, who had rejected farming as a way of life, was eager to embrace this new industrial order personally and politically. Jefferson's prediction that the United States would remain a nation of independent farmers was turning out to be inaccurate. But even Jefferson, when he became president of the United States, was sensing that his national model of independent farmers might need some modification. In 1808, Jefferson's secretary of the treasury, Albert Gallatin, proposed a federally funded network of roads and canals that would "shorten the distances into the remote corners of the United States."[12] The new nation was expanding as citizens moved across the country seeking new places to live and work, and these places needed to be connected to keep the nation united.

Gallatin's notion was on target. To make this new industrial economy work, internal improvements—what might be called infrastructure projects in the twenty-first century—were necessary. Roads, railroads, bridges, canals, harbors, and dams needed to be constructed or upgraded to facilitate the efficient creation and the shipping of manufactured products around the nation. Natural environments would have to be altered, even subdued, in this construction effort. Rivers were already being dammed in New England around textile mills. Railroads would have to slice through forests and public lands to make way for the laying of tracks. To facilitate steamboat travel, rivers would have to be dredged, and canals would have to be dug to connect waterways, which involved damming waters, creating lakes and ponds where none previously existed, and digging new channels for flowing waters. As one twenty-first-century environmental historian put it, canals were "artificial rivers" that "epitomized nineteenth-century notions of improving and commanding nature."[13]

In 1817, the state of New York began one of these internal improvements that inspired the rest of the nation. With enthusiastic support from Governor DeWitt Clinton, New York funded and commenced the construction of the Erie Canal, a 360-mile waterway that would connect the Hudson River at Albany to Lake Erie. Construction took eight years—during which time it was labeled "Clinton's Folly" by the governor's political opponents—but when it opened, the Erie Canal reduced shipping time between those two locations, which were not yet connected by railroads, from thirty to eight days and reduced shipping costs by 85 percent, which could sharply reduce the prices of consumer products transported along the canal.[14] New York City, at the mouth of the Hudson River, was now connected by waterways to Lake Erie. New York added the Oswego Canal in 1828, extending the reach of the Erie Canal to Lake Ontario.

The next chapter in Lincoln's environmental biography depicts him as an enthusiastic political supporter of these efforts to reshape the natural environment with the internal improvements needed to fuel the Industrial Revolution. When Lincoln began his political career in the Illinois legislature during the 1830s, the Whig Party, led by Henry Clay of Kentucky, was already forming as a pro–internal improvements political party. Lincoln was eager to affiliate with the Whigs, and Clay became his political idol. Lincoln's first published political statement in 1832 had been a call for reshaping the Sangamon River to facilitate steamboat travel. Now, in the Illinois legislature, he found himself among a large cohort of like-minded colleagues.

Their state was perfectly suited for infrastructure improvements. The natural landscape of Illinois is mostly flat. Roads and railroads did not have to scale or circumvent major mountain ranges nor cross wide canyons. A sizable portion of the Illinois landscape was open prairie rather than woodlands, which meant that forests would not have to be cleared to make space for railroad tracks.[15] The Illinois Whigs strongly advocated that both state and federal land be made available for the construction of roads, canals, bridges, and railroads and that state funding also be made available for this purpose. According to the Whigs, tax dollars used for internal improvements would be money wisely spent. The improvements would pay off with increased business and trade, which would benefit all Illinois residents. Lincoln, whose life on farms had often put him at the mercy of nature, had now joined a group of lawmakers who were enthusiastically working to shape the natural environment to fit the needs of citizens.

Two weeks after Lincoln took his seat in the Illinois legislature, in December 1834, he introduced a bill to authorize Samuel Musick, an Illinois resident, to build and operate a toll bridge across Salt Creek in Sangamon County.[16] Over the next two years, Lincoln sponsored or supported several bills proposing the creation of a system of state roads. In December 1835, he sponsored a resolution to incorporate a company to create a canal in the Sangamon River valley. The following year, Lincoln and other Illinois lawmakers also enthusiastically supported an ambitious plan to provide state funding for a canal that would connect the Illinois and Chicago Rivers. This canal would link Lake Michigan and the city of Chicago on its shores to the Mississippi River, enabling the efficient shipping of Illinois products southward. According to his friend Joshua Speed, Lincoln's "highest ambition was to become the DeWitt Clinton of Ill[inoi]s" at this time of his life.[17] Construction of the Illinois and Michigan Canal began in 1836, but a national financial crisis, referred to as the Panic of 1837, caused financing issues that halted construction. In January 1840, Lincoln addressed the Illinois legislature, urging continuation of the work and completion of the canal. Discontinuing work on the canal, in Lincoln's view, was "very much like stopping a skift in the middle of a river—if it was not going up, it *would* go down. The embankments upon the Canal would be washing away, and the excavations filling up."[18] The canal was eventually completed in 1848.

Like other Illinois Whigs, Lincoln favored the purchase of federal lands by the state of Illinois, which would then sell those lands to fund the state's internal improvements. In a committee report to the Illinois assembly delivered in January 1839, Lincoln stressed the importance of funding the state's ambitious internal improvement projects. "In the first place, then, we are now so far advanced in a general system of internal improvements that, if we would, we cannot retreat from it, without disgrace and great loss. The conclusion then is, that we *must* advance," he stated. The sale of public lands acquired from the federal government by Illinois "will pay the interest on the loan created for their own purchase, and also [the interest] upon many millions of our internal improvement loans."[19]

While serving in the Illinois assembly, Lincoln consistently encouraged the acquisition of lands for railroads. He enthusiastically supported state funding to assist in the construction of a railroad running from Alton, Illinois, a town on the Mississippi River, through the capital city of Springfield to the eastern boundary of Illinois. That plan was initially funded but later halted. Even after he left the Illinois legislature—he did not seek reelection in 1842—Lincoln continued to be a voice urging the construction of that railroad as a key to the state's economic prosperity. In August 1847, he joined a Sangamon County citizens group to urge the creation of the Alton and Springfield Railroad. In a report directed toward Illinois lawmakers and appearing in the *Sangamo Journal*, Lincoln's committee stated, "Constructing a rail road from Alton to Springfield, is viewed but as a link in a great chain of rail road communication which shall unite Boston and New York with the Mississippi [River]."[20] Railroads, like canals, could facilitate trade between the East and the Midwest by shortening travel time between the two regions.

Lincoln won a seat as a Whig in the U.S. House of Representatives in 1846. During his single term in Congress, he continued to be a voice for internal improvements. In June 1847, Lincoln delivered a long speech in the House of Representatives on "the general subject of internal improvements." Unlike Lincoln's Whig Party, Democrats in

Congress had not been supportive of internal improvements, arguing that the U.S. Constitution did not authorize the federal government to develop such projects, such projects were too costly, and they benefited only the citizens directly served by those improvements rather than the entire nation. In his speech, Lincoln tried to refute each of these opposing arguments. He asserted that the federal government could control the costs of internal improvement projects so as not to break the Treasury. He likened the spending of federal funds for internal improvements to Congress's funding of the U.S. Navy. Just as the navy protects American shipping "by driving a pirate [ship] from the track of commerce on the broad ocean," a federally funded river project can augment commerce by "removing a snag from it's more narrow path in the Mississippi river. . . . Each is done to save life and property, and for nothing else." Lincoln offered the newly opened Illinois and Michigan Canal as a prime example of how a local internal improvement project could profit the entire nation. "Every inch of it [the canal] is within the state of Illinois," he stated, but within days of the canal's opening, "sugar had been carried from New-Orleans through this canal to Buffalo in New-York." As a result, "the New Orleans merchant sold his sugar a little *dearer;* and the people of Buffalo sweetened their coffee a little *cheaper.*" The benefit was not to Illinois, "where the canal *is,* but to Louisiana and New-York, where it is *not.*" Lincoln also cited legal texts to defend the constitutionality of securing federal funding for internal improvements.[21]

Lincoln served only one term in Congress. When his term ended in 1849, before he left Washington to return to Springfield, Lincoln applied for a patent. The problem he faced in his first infrastructure project in New Salem, Illinois, in 1831, altering the shape and flow of the Sangamon River to facilitate the movement of larger vessels, had remained on his mind. On March 10, 1849, Lincoln applied for, and later received, a patent for a device that could lift boats over river shoals. When large, heavily burdened boats came to a shallow section of a river or a sandbar, the boat's cargo would usually have to be removed, and the boat would have to be forced through the shallow channel, then reloaded, a process requiring both time and labor, thereby increasing transportation costs. Lincoln's invention offered "a new and improved manner of combining adjustable buoyant air chambers with a steam boat or other vessel for the purpose of enabling their draught of water to be readily lessened to enable them to pass over bars, or through shallow water, without discharging their cargoes."[22] Lincoln's patent, however, was never used commercially.

Lincoln took a political sabbatical after his term in Congress, focusing on his legal career, but he continued to be involved with and to advocate for internal improvements. When he returned to Illinois, a railroad commencing in Chicago and winding southward had been established. Lincoln began representing Illinois railroads as an attorney. His first major railroad case was in 1851, and he began doing legal work for the Illinois Central Railroad the following year. Railroad companies often required legal assistance. They needed to acquire parcels of land for tracks and stations, and lawsuits were frequently filed by farmers alleging that railroad companies were adversely affecting farmland or killing or blocking the movement of livestock and by small towns trying to block railroad construction. From 1852 until 1860, when he was elected president, Lincoln represented Illinois railroads in fifty cases, though he also represented individuals who were suing railroad companies. His railroad cases were the most lucrative of his legal career; the case of *Illinois Central Railroad v. McLean County* was Lincoln's single most remunerative law case.[23]

Despite his profitable legal career, Lincoln returned to politics in 1854, after the passage of the Kansas-Nebraska Act brought the issue of slavery in the U.S. territories to the national forefront. He became a leader in Illinois of the anti-Nebraska movement, and he joined the Republican Party, which formed in 1854 as an antislavery party. Lincoln's bids for a seat in the U.S. Senate in 1855 and 1858 both failed, but Lincoln was elected president in 1860. The Civil War and the issue of slavery were monumental political problems with which Lincoln had to grapple during his entire presidency, but he continued to devote attention to his very first political issue, internal improvements. The Whigs had failed as a party in 1854, fractured over the slavery issue, but internal improvements remained on the national agenda and in Lincoln's mind. He supported the expansion of New York's Erie and Oswego Canals.

The infrastructure project to which he devoted the most attention as president was the transcontinental railroad, a line that would connect the railroad network of the Midwest with that of the Far West; it would enable a passenger to board a train in St. Louis or Chicago and travel to San Francisco, across the Rocky Mountains. In his annual message to Congress on December 1, 1862, delivered at a time when the war was raging and the issue of emancipating the slaves topped his political agenda, Lincoln spoke of the need to continue internal improvement projects. He noted the progress of the transcontinental railroad and requested "the favorable action of Congress upon the projects now pending before them for enlarging the capacities of the great canals in New York and Illinois." Such projects, asserted Lincoln, were "vital, and [of] rapidly increasing importance to the whole nation, and especially to the vast interior region."[24]

New modes of transportation were not the only element of the new American industrial order to gain Lincoln's attention. Lincoln and other Whigs, and later the Republicans, were staunch supporters of American manufacturing. They attempted to create a climate that fostered an industrial economy that produced goods being demanded by American consumers so that these products would not have to be imported. In March 1843, after his term in the Illinois legislature had ended, Lincoln joined two other Illinois Whigs to compose a circular for the forthcoming political campaign that affirmed the party's strong support for manufacturing. The circular included a quote from an 1816 letter in support of manufacturing authored by Thomas Jefferson. Jefferson had labeled American agriculture the bedrock of democracy, but several years after his presidency, he had begun to recognize the need for a manufacturing economy in the United States:

> To be independent for the comforts of life, we must fabricate them ourselves. We must now place the manufacturer by the side of the agriculturalist. The grand jury now is, shall we make our own comforts, or go without them at the will of a foreign nation? He, therefore, who is now against domestic manufactures must be for reducing us either to dependence on that

foreign nation, or to be clothed in skins and to live like wild beasts in dens and caverns. I am not one of those; experience has taught me that manufactures are now as necessary to our independence as to our comfort.[25]

Jefferson, the staunch advocate for American agriculture, had come to realize that to sustain American democracy, the United States must manufacture its own products rather than depend on imports from other nations. The same 1843 Whig circular that included Jefferson's quote also included one from a letter written in 1824 by former president Andrew Jackson. Jackson stated that "there is too much labor employed in agriculture." Because the country does not manufacture its own goods, "we have been too long subject to the policy of British merchants."[26] To become truly independent, the United States must invent and produce its own consumer products, not rely on producers and merchants from abroad.

During his prepresidential years, while still living in Illinois, Lincoln delivered two lectures on discoveries and inventions, one to the Young Men's Association of Bloomington, Illinois, in April 1858 and a second ten months later for the Phi Alpha Society of Illinois College in Jacksonville, Illinois. He delivered the second lecture at other venues in Illinois as well. "Man is not the only animal who labors; but he is the only one who *improves* his workmanship. This improvement, he effects by *Discoveries*, and *Inventions*," he asserted in the first lecture.[27] That first lecture examined discoveries and inventions of the ancient world—clothing, the wheel and cart, the plow. The second lecture highlighted some of the recent inventions that were transforming what Lincoln called "Young America." He noted the creation of the steam engine, which resulted in the invention of the steamboat and the railroad. Lincoln proudly asserted that the United States was ahead of countries in Europe and Asia in the development of new inventions: "We, here in America, *think* we discover, and invent, and improve, faster than any of them. *They* may think this is arrogance; but they can not deny that Russia has called on us to show her how to build steam-boats and railroads—while in the older parts of Asia, they scarcely know that such things as S.Bs & RRs exist."

Lincoln saw "the discovery of America as an event greatly favoring and facilitating useful discoveries and inventions."[28]

Several months after delivering this second lecture on discoveries and inventions, Lincoln spoke at the Wisconsin State Agricultural Society in Milwaukee and expressed the need to increase per-acre yields by improving agricultural methods. One method to achieve this goal would be to integrate new machine technology into agriculture. Specifically, Lincoln urged the "successful application of *steam power*, to farm work . . . especially a Steam Plow." Such a plow would "afford an advantage over plowing with animals." Lincoln outlined the many difficulties in designing a steam plow, but he expressed confidence that "ingenious men" would be able to overcome those difficulties. "It is to be hoped that the steam plow will be finally successful," Lincoln stated, "producing the largest crop possible from a given quantity of ground."[29] Thus the technology and products of the Industrial Revolution could enhance agriculture, enabling farmers to reap more from their environmental landscapes.

Another key invention that was sweeping across the nation in the 1850s was the telegraph, developed in America in 1847 by Samuel Morse. Like the steamboat and the locomotive, the telegraph shrunk the distance between two points by enabling almost instant communication. Before the telegraph, messages in hard copy had to be shipped to their destinations by boat, train, horse, stagecoach, or other horse-drawn vehicle. Lincoln certainly learned the power of the telegraph when he ran for an Illinois U.S. Senate seat in 1858. His lengthy debates with his Democratic opponent, Stephen Douglas, were recorded and telegraphed across the nation, then printed in newspapers for readers. The printed debates gave Lincoln a national name and audience. When he ran for president two years later, his persona and his views were familiar to many voters across the nation who had followed the Lincoln-Douglas debates in their local newspapers. Later, as president, Lincoln made extensive use of the telegraph, which was especially efficient at communicating war news from battlefronts to the War Department in Washington, where Lincoln could frequently be seen reading the dispatches. Lincoln strongly supported the creation of a trans-Atlantic telegraph line that would connect the United States and Great Britain.[30]

Lincoln's interest in new inventions continued for the rest of his life. As president, he was especially interested in new weaponry that could be employed by the Union army in the war effort. Lincoln was frequently visited in the White House by inventors detailing or demonstrating new weapons—cannons, rifles, balls and shells, even a submarine. Often Lincoln sampled a model rifle before sending the visitor to meet his secretary of war or military commanders under whose watch the proposed weapons would undergo closer examination and field testing.

To encourage the development of more inventions as well as their manufacture, Lincoln and the Whig Party, and later the Republicans, advocated a protective tariff on imported goods, a key proposal in Hamilton and Coxe's 1791 report. Such a tariff would raise the price of imported consumer products and foster the creation and sale of cheaper, American-made products. Lincoln spoke consistently on the need for a tariff throughout his political career. During the 1840s and 1850s, Lincoln signed numerous resolutions and spoke in favor of Whig Party platforms advocating a protective tariff. When the Whig Party dissipated in 1854 and Lincoln became a Republican, he continued to support his former party's platform plank on tariffs. Writing to a potential Republican supporter in Pennsylvania in 1859, Lincoln stated, "I was an old Henry Clay tariff whig. In the old times I made more speeches on that subject, than on any other. I have not since changed my views. I believe yet, if we could have a moderate, carefully adjusted, protective tariff, so far acquiesced in, as to not be a perpetual subject of political strife, squabbles, charges, and uncertainties, it would be better for us."[31]

Traveling by train to Washington for his presidential inauguration, Lincoln delivered a speech at a stop in Pittsburgh, which was already heavily involved in iron and tin production, and he highlighted the tariff issue as one on which his administration would focus. He promised his listeners that he would carefully study the tariff issue "so that when the time for action arrives adequate protection can be extended to the coal and iron of Pennsylvania, the corn of Illinois, and the 'reapers of Chicago.'" The needs of no section of the nation would be overlooked, "but that all sections may share in common the benefits of a just and equitable tariff."[32] These key benefits would be more American inventions, more consumer products, and more vehicles for shipping these products across the nation more efficiently. This Industrial Revolution was, in Lincoln's view, benefiting the entire nation.

Before he became president, however, neither Lincoln nor his like-minded political allies seemed to consider how this new industrial order that benefited so many Americans might affect the American natural environment. But even before Slater built his mill on the Blackstone River in Pawtucket, Rhode Island, a handful of British critics, including the Scottish philosopher and writer Thomas Carlyle, were highlighting the negative environmental effects of their country's new factory system. In the view of these critics, as factories appeared, too many environmental landscapes had become ugly, losing their natural beauty. Workers in Great Britain's textile mills were living divorced from the natural environment, which was fast disappearing.[33]

Industrialization would affect the American landscape as well. Even Slater's modest 1790 Rhode Island mill was having a serious local environmental impact. Before the arrival of Slater's dam, Rhode Island farmers supplemented their diet with salmon and shad, anadromous fish that lived in salt water but journeyed upstream through the Blackstone River into freshwater rivers and lakes to spawn. This annual freshwater fish migration took place in the late spring, shortly after the yearly planting of new crops that would not be ripe for picking and consumption until later in the summer. The fish were a major source of preharvest protein for farmers, and fish remains were a fertilizer for their farm fields. In colonial times, local lawmakers had empowered these Rhode Island farmers by passing a series of Fish Acts authorizing the removal of dams that blocked migratory fish. Hence, the owners of dams, which were smaller before the erection of Slater's dam, created fish passages around the dams for migratory fish, enabling them to swim upstream to spawn and enabling local farmers to catch the fish and bring them to their dinner tables. By the time Slater built his dam in 1790, however, Rhode Island mill operators had begun to gain political power at the expense of local farmers. Laws protecting fish migrations disappeared. In 1792, Rhode Island farmers petitioned the state's general assembly to close Slater's dam so that the salmon would return, but Slater had great political influence and persuaded lawmakers to deny the farmers' request. Over the next thirty years, other textile mills with large dams like Slater's began to appear along Rhode Island rivers. By the middle of the nineteenth century, the salmon were gone.[34]

The same phenomenon was soon occurring throughout coastal New England. The first New England dams, powering sawmills and gristmills, were modest in size. Many operated in the fall, after the harvest season, so the dam gates could be left open in the spring and not impede the annual upstream migration of anadromous fish. But the new factories and mills that fueled the American Industrial Revolution—Massachusetts and New Hampshire textile mills and blast furnaces that were cranking out iron for the construction of Lincoln's beloved railroads—were larger, needed more energy, and operated throughout the year. Salmon and shad were quickly disappearing from New England rivers.[35] The mills also polluted fish habitats with dyes, wood pulp, and sulfuric acid.[36]

Henry David Thoreau, born in 1817, was growing into adulthood as the economic and natural landscape of his native New England was undergoing the changes wrought by industrialization, and he began to write critically about what he witnessed. One scholar of American nature writing appropriately calls Thoreau "the patron saint of environmental writing."[37] In 1839, Thoreau and his brother, John, took a boat trip from Concord, Massachusetts, where they lived, to Concord, New Hampshire. During their weeklong journey, the Thoreau brothers traveled the Concord River, Middlesex Canal, and Merrimack River. In 1849, Henry David Thoreau published a short book on his experience, *A Week on the Concord and Merrimack Rivers.* Thoreau commented on the disappearance of anadromous fish in the Concord River: "Salmon, shad, and alewives were formerly abundant here . . . used as food and manure, until the dam and afterward the canal at Billerica, and the factories at Lowell, put an end to their migration hitherward." "Poor shad!" lamented Thoreau. "Still wandering the sea in thy scaly armor to inquire humbly at the mouth of rivers if man has perchance left them free to enter." Nonetheless, Thoreau was guardedly optimistic about the fish's long-term future. Sarcastically, he wrote, "Perchance after a few thousands of years, if the fish will be patient, and pass their summers elsewhere meanwhile, nature will have leveled the Billerica dam, and the Lowell factories, and the Grass-ground River run clear again." Thoreau hinted at a more immediate remedy for the shad's problem: "Who knows what may avail a crowbar against that Billerica dam?"[38] Perhaps some farmers took Thoreau's crowbar solution seriously. In the late 1850s, a group of New Hampshire farmers, under the direction of James Worster, began destroying dams that had caused flooding in nearby farm fields.[39]

At this time, Lincoln, who never met Thoreau and probably did not read anything that Thoreau wrote,[40] likely did not consider the impact that the damming of rivers would have on anadromous fish. Lincoln grew to adulthood in the Midwest, far removed from the annual salmon and shad migrations about which Thoreau was writing. For Lincoln, the damming of rivers was necessary to power the mills that created the materials and goods that fueled the Industrial Revolution. At the time that Thoreau was writing, the preservation of East Coast fish habitats was not on Lincoln's, or the Whig Party's, political agenda.

Rivers were not the only element of the natural landscape affected by the Industrial Revolution. Forests also suffered. Deforestation was already a serious environmental problem in New England at the beginning of the eighteenth century. The farming methods practiced in New England at the time, and later duplicated in the South and Lincoln's Midwest, began the deforestation process. Farmers like the Lincolns initially chopped trees or burned sections of woodlands to create their farm fields. After several growing seasons, the fields, without fertilizers, became infertile, and new farm fields had to be carved out of the woodlands. Lincoln, so handy with an ax, participated in this type of agricultural deforestation during his years on family farms.

Crops such as tobacco, grown mainly in the upper South but also in the Mid-Atlantic region and New England, and cotton, grown mainly in the lower South, were particularly hard on the soil. By the late eighteenth century, some of the more affluent plantation owners, such as George Washington, Thomas Jefferson, and James Madison, were experimenting with crop rotation to preserve soils. Edmund Ruffin, a Virginian later known for allegedly firing the first shot of the Civil War and committing suicide after the North's victory, published a book on soil fertilization in 1832, titled *An Essay on Calcareous Manures*.[41] But by the time the use of soil fertilizers, other than livestock manure and fish remains, became widespread, serious deforestation already had taken place. Farmers also used trees to create posts and rails to fence in livestock and as fuel for cooking and heating. In 1830, 95 percent of the nation's energy needs were supplied by wood.[42]

The New England lumber business also contributed to deforestation. The overwhelming majority of buildings constructed in colonial New England were made of wood chopped from local forests and processed by hand and later in sawmills for construction. As early as 1609, a shipload of New England lumber was sent to Great Britain for ship construction. By this time, Great Britain had suffered from deforestation, and its shipbuilders began to rely on pines chopped down in New England to serve as masts.[43] In colonial times, the forests of North America might have appeared to be endless, but by the early nineteenth century, they had become much sparser and some had even disappeared, especially those along the East Coast. The lumbering industry, still one of the most important in the United States in the late eighteenth and early nineteenth centuries, moved westward to the Great Lakes region and eventually farther west during Lincoln's lifetime. Deforestation also contributed to soil infertility, as nutrients from tree leaves served as a natural fertilizer. When forests vanished, birds and wildlife also often disappeared.[44] In an essay titled "Walking," published in 1862, Thoreau wrote, "We are accustomed to say in New England that fewer and fewer pigeons visit us every year. Our forests furnish no masts for them."[45]

Forests were also cleared in mining operations. Iron and other metals were key elements in many of the new manufactured products whose production was so strongly encouraged and supported by Lincoln and his Whig Party. Mining towns, which, like factory towns, proliferated during the Industrial Revolution, often lacked trees and other natural flora. Blast furnaces, used in the production of iron, typically consumed two-plus acres of trees per day.[46] By the late 1840s, deforestation in New England was noticeable to some observers. According to an 1847 article in *Harbinger* magazine titled "Trip to Vermont," "The beautiful pastoral life of the inhabitants will give place to oppressive factory village life—quiet, rural pursuits will be absorbed in the din, conflict and degradation of manufacturing and mechanical business."[47] But few individuals or political leaders realized what Thoreau and others had grasped—that America's plentiful forests, by the mid-nineteenth century, were becoming seriously depleted.

The transportation devices of the new industrial order that were so beloved by Lincoln and his Whig Party also had an impact on the American environment. Steamboats ran on wood, as did locomotives, until coal later became a fuel. Railroads used wood in almost every part of their operation. As one twenty-first-century environmental historian put it, railroads had "a hunger for trees."[48] Forests had to be cleared to lay down tracks. Rails were held together with wooden ties, and wooden bridges were erected to enable railroads to pass over rivers and canyons. Railroads also polluted landscapes with smoke and ashes; sometimes hot ashes and embers from locomotives were released into the landscape, causing forest fires. In the Great Plains, trains were partly responsible for the great reduction in buffalo herds.[49] Trains, especially after coal became a primary fuel source, also caused air pollution and noise pollution.[50] Writing in *Walden*, his 1854 chronicle of his twenty-six-month stay during the 1840s in a one-room cabin in Walden Woods in Concord, Massachusetts, Thoreau described the noise of a locomotive announcing itself as it passed by: "The whistle of the locomotive penetrates my woods summer and winter, sounding like the scream of a hawk sailing over some farmer's yard, informing me that many restless city merchants are arriving within the circle of the town, or adventurous country traders from the other side." He described the passing train ominously, as a "travelling demigod" with its "steam cloud like a banner streaming behind," making "the hills echo with his snort like thunder, shaking the earth with his feet, and breathing fire and smoke from his nostrils."[51]

For Lincoln, that train rambling through the countryside, carrying passengers and products, would be a welcome sight, a striking symbol of the new American industrial order. Lincoln was part of an extensive nationwide effort to transform the American natural landscape, to reshape it to facilitate the creation and transportation of the country's manufactured products. Factories, dams, canals, harbors, roads, bridges, and railroads would reshape the American natural landscape into one very different from the rural landscape in which Lincoln had grown to adulthood. Not until a year or two into his presidency would Lincoln begin to consider some of the negative effects of industrialization on the American natural environment and develop some political strategies for dealing with those effects.

MY CHILDHOOD-HOME I SEE AGAIN

I n his early adulthood, Abraham Lincoln made a determined attempt to minimize his direct contact with and vulnerability to
the natural environment by leaving his family's farm, becoming an
attorney, and later, entering politics and embracing the Whig agenda
of internal improvements. But spiritually and psychologically, Lincoln remained, in some way, connected to the natural environment
in which he was raised. In the fall of 1844, Lincoln, while living and
working as an attorney in Springfield, Illinois, made a trip to Indiana.
On October 30, he delivered a speech in Rockport, Indiana, on behalf
of Whig presidential candidate Henry Clay and other Whigs running
for political office. Lincoln's speech stressed a key item on the Whig
political agenda—the need for a protective tariff on imported goods.

While in Indiana, Lincoln made a visit to his boyhood home.
His family had moved from Kentucky to Little Pigeon Creek, Indiana, in 1816, when Abraham was seven years old, and the Lincolns
lived in Indiana until 1830, when they relocated to Illinois. When
he returned in 1844 to the site of his family's former Indiana farm,
Lincoln, now thirty-five years old, traversed the natural landscape on
which he had spent part of his boyhood, and he visited his mother's
grave. Not surprisingly, the trip triggered nostalgia and bittersweet
childhood memories. At some point, Lincoln began composing a
poem about his Indiana visit. Sixteen months later, Lincoln, back in
Springfield, sent a letter to his friend Andrew Johnston. "Feeling a
little poetic this evening," Lincoln wrote, "I have concluded to redeem

my promise this evening by sending you the piece you expressed the wish to have. You find it enclosed." The enclosed piece was a copy of "Mortality" by the Scottish poet William Knox, a melancholy poem stressing the mortality of all living creatures. The letter to Johnston also made reference to a poem that Lincoln was composing: "By the way, how would you like to see a piece of poetry of my own making? I have a piece that is almost done, but I find a great deal of trouble to finish it."[1] Over the next several months, Lincoln sent pieces of his unfinished poem to Johnston.

Lincoln's poem was titled "My Childhood-Home I See Again," referring to the visit that he had made to his boyhood homestead in Indiana in the fall of 1844. An early draft of the poem, still apparently unfinished, comprised twenty-four stanzas, each consisting of four lines in an *abab* rhyme scheme, a line with eight beats followed by one with six beats. Several verses of the poem record the woes of Lincoln's boyhood friend Matthew, who, "Once of genius bright," was "Now locked for aye, in mental night, / A haggard mad-man wild." The bulk of the poem, however, conveys Lincoln's bittersweet sense of nostalgia for his childhood world now forever lost. The poem opens:

> My childhood-home I see again,
>   And gladden with the view;
> And still as mem'ries crowd my brain
>   There's sadness in it too.

The poem relies on nature similes to convey the speaker's feelings about his past:

> As distant mountains please the eye,
>   When twilight chases day—
> As bugle-tones, that, passing by,
>   In distance die away—
> As leaving some grand water-fall
>   We ling'ring, list it's roar,
> So memory will hallow all
>   We've known, but know no more.

> Now twenty years have passed away,
>> Since here I bid farewell
> To woods, and fields, and scenes of play
>> And school-mates loved so well.

The speaker, reimagining his past, "range[s] the fields with pensive tread, / And pace[s] the hollow rooms." The last stanza of this apparently unfinished poem suggests the speaker's sense that he is still connected, in some spiritual way, to the land that he farmed as a child and young man:

> The very spot where grew the bread
>> That formed my bones, I see.
> How strange, old field, on thee to tread,
>> And feel I'm part of thee![2]

One twenty-first-century critical analysis of Lincoln's verses suggests that the poem records its speaker's "fear of being drawn down toward the cold and static world of the dead" and "being caught again in the 'hollow rooms' of a childhood that never seemed to have enough mental stimulation or enough educational opportunity to fulfill young Lincoln's aspirations. It is the psychological tomb of his father's illiteracy and his subsistence farming that Lincoln's speaker fears as much as anything else." The poem conveys "a deeply personal grief" but also emphasizes "the strong ties between the poem's speaker and the natural world."[3] That analysis squares with what some Lincoln scholars have suggested regarding Lincoln's ties to the natural landscape of his youth. As one scholar wrote, "Although words printed on leaves of paper increasingly absorbed his [Lincoln's] attention, the nature that lay beyond them—the nature of water, earth, plants, and fish—continued to shape him."[4] Lincoln's autobiographical poem suggests that those old farm fields that he trod as a child and young man remained, in some way, a fundamental part of him, despite his attempt to distance himself from them physically and emotionally.

In September 1848, four years after he made the trip to Indiana that triggered the composition of "My Childhood-Home I See Again," while he was serving in the House of Representatives, Lincoln decided to take a long, circuitous route back to Illinois during a congressional recess. Mary Lincoln accompanied him. From Washington, the Lincolns headed to Massachusetts, where Lincoln spent two weeks campaigning for Whig candidates. Then the Lincolns traveled to Albany, New York, where they boarded a train for Buffalo and headed home to Illinois. On the way home from Buffalo, the Lincolns stopped to see Niagara Falls. Lincoln had traveled on the mighty Mississippi River on the two flatboat trips that he had made to New Orleans as a young man. The year before he visited Niagara Falls, he had traveled to Chicago for the first time and saw majestic Lake Michigan. But Lincoln was not so taken by the Mississippi River or Lake Michigan that he felt compelled to describe either of them in writing. Niagara Falls was different. After seeing the falls, Lincoln felt the urge, probably shortly afterward, to record his observations in writing—this time using prose, not poetry.

Sometime after Lincoln returned to Springfield, his law partner, William Herndon, also made a trip to Niagara Falls. In his 1888 biography of Lincoln, Herndon reported what happened after the two attorneys met in their office after Herndon's return:

> In the office, a few days after my return, I was endeavoring to entertain my partner with an account of my trip, and among other things described the Falls. In the attempt I indulged in a good deal of imagery. As I warmed up with the subject my descriptive powers expanded accordingly. The mad rush of water, the roar, the rapids, and the rainbow furnished me with an abundance of material for a stirring and impressive picture. The recollection of the gigantic and awe-inspiring scene stimulated my exuberant powers to the highest pitch.

But when Herndon asked Lincoln for his own impressions of Niagara Falls, Lincoln stated, "'The thing that struck me most forcibly when I saw the Falls . . . was where in the world did all that water come from?'" According to Herndon, Lincoln "had no eye for the magnificence and grandeur of the scene, for the rapids, the mist, the angry waters, and the roar of the whirlpool, but his mind, working in its accustomed channel, heedless of beauty or awe, followed irresistibly back to the first cause."[5]

Herndon was wrong. The "magnificence and grandeur of the scene" had certainly made an impression on Lincoln. After his visit to Niagara Falls, Lincoln, probably unbeknownst to Herndon, penned a two-paragraph description of the falls that could have been written by Henry David Thoreau or another American transcendentalist writer of the time. First, Lincoln described the physical elements of the scene:

> There is no mystery about the thing itself. Every effect is just such as any intelligent man knowing the causes, would anticipate, without [seeing] it. If the water moving onward in a great river, reaches a point where there is a perpendicular jog, of a hundred feet in descent, in the bottom of the river,
> —it is plain the water will have a violent and continuous plunge at that point. It is also plain the water, thus plunging, will foam, and roar, and send up a mist, continuously, in which last, during sunshine, there will be perpetual rain-bows.

Then Lincoln's description moved beyond the purely physical: "The mere physical of Niagara Falls is only this. Yet this is really a very small part of that world's wonder. It's power to excite reflection, and emotion, is it's great charm." Lincoln noted how a geologist or a philosopher might view the falls, then added his own reflection: "But still there is more. It calls up the indefinite past." When Columbus discovered the American continent, when Christ died on the cross, when Moses parted the Red Sea, when Adam of the book of Genesis came to life, "then as now, Niagara was roaring here." The mammoth and mastodon, long gone, "have gazed on Niagara. In that long—long time, never still for a single moment. Never dried, never froze, never slept, never rested,"[6] The description concluded with that comma, suggesting that Lincoln meant to continue writing, perhaps explaining in more dctail the endurance of nature, symbolized by the great falls, through human history. But apparently, Lincoln never continued or completed the piece.

The Niagara Falls description, like "My Childhood-Home I See Again," indicates that Lincoln had not completely divorced himself from the natural landscape. He had physically escaped from the rugged natural environment of his youth and young adulthood; he no longer worked within it or lived so directly at its mercy. But many years later, Lincoln retained more than a passing nostalgia for the natural world; it still affected him in a meaningful way. The visit to his childhood home provoked Lincoln to consider how his past experiences in the natural environment might have shaped him. The visit to Niagara Falls prompted within him thoughts about the temporality of human beings and the abiding quality of the natural world. An examination of Lincoln's writings and speeches, over many years, suggests that the natural landscapes of his youth formed an important part of his biography that remained with him in some fundamental ways throughout his lifetime, readily available for retrieval.

Like the gentlemen depicted in this image, Abraham Lincoln was mesmerized by the natural beauty of Niagara Falls. After his visit, he penned a moving description of the falls. Library of Congress.

Even before Lincoln became a great speaker and writer, however, he was, according to many friends and colleagues, a superb storyteller. As a child, Lincoln loved to hear and tell stories. His father had been a good storyteller. The literary and debating club that he had joined as a young man when he moved to New Salem was undoubtedly a forum for storytelling. During downtime between legislative sessions in the Illinois assembly, the assemblymen told stories. Later, when Lincoln began working in Illinois as an attorney, he rode the judicial circuit with other attorneys—judges traveled through the state holding court sessions, and a group of attorneys followed the judges to try those cases. In the evenings, after the court had adjourned for the day, the attorneys gathered in eateries, taverns, and lodging places; discussed the day's judicial proceedings; and swapped stories. The attorneys entertained each other by telling stories, and Lincoln was reportedly very good at it. "He was always full of his Stories," John Hanks, Lincoln's mother's cousin, said about him, "as much so in Indiana as Ill[inoi]s."[7] "No man could tell a story as well as he could," stated Joseph Gillespie, who served with Lincoln in the Illinois general assembly. "He could convey his ideas on any subject through the form of a simple story or homely illustration with better effect than any man I ever knew."[8] Lincoln continued to use stories to entertain, make a point, or persuade a listener throughout his legal and political career.

Many of Lincoln's best stories relied on analogies and metaphors from the natural world and from his early life on farms. For example, in the 1840s, Lincoln's radical political opponents in the Democratic Party were often called "Locofocos" by the Whigs. (The term came from a kind of match that these Democrats used to light candles during a meeting after the meeting room's gaslights were turned off.) To illustrate the caginess of these Locofocos, Lincoln told his political comrades the story of a farmer who finds a polecat in his barn threatening his chickens. The polecat tries to assure the farmer that he is really a friend of the chickens, staying in the barn only to protect them. The farmer says, "You look like a polecat, just the size of a polecat, act like one . . . and smell like one, and you are one, by God, and I'll kill you, innocent and as friendly to me as you say you are." Lincoln then offered the meaning of his tale: "These Locofocos claim to be true Democrats, but they are only Locofocos. They look like Locofocos, just the size of Locofocos, act like Locofocos, and . . . are Locofocos, by God." Speaking to a small audience in Kansas in 1859, Lincoln used a farming anecdote to criticize the Democratic Party's meanderings on the slavery question. Lincoln spoke of a boy plowing a field who asked his father in what direction he should form a new fallow. The father told the boy to aim for a yoke of oxen standing at the other end of the field. The father left, and the oxen began to roam around the field. The boy plowed with his eye fixed on the oxen and created a circular furrow instead of one in a straight line. So, too, had the Democrats, in Lincoln's view, wandered on the important issue of slavery.[9]

During the Civil War, Lincoln, as president and commander in chief, often used anecdotes from the natural world to explain military and political strategy, clarify his political positions, and pose or solve problems. For example, speaking to a political supporter in 1864, Lincoln discussed an Ohio Democratic congressman, Samuel S. Cox, nicknamed "Sunset" or "Sunny," who, though a member of the opposing political party, still claimed loyalty to Lincoln and the Union. Lincoln explained that Congressman Cox was like an old sow that had run off the farm and been missing for a few days. The farmer summoned his two sons to help him find the sow. He assumed that the sow was near the creek feeding on the ironweeds. The farmer told his sons, "Now you go over the creek and go down that side of it, and I'll go down this side and we'll find her, for I believe she is on both sides of the creek." Like the sow, Lincoln concluded, "Sunny is trying to be on both sides of the creek."[10]

Sometime after the Lincoln administration imposed a military draft to enlist badly needed recruits for the Union army, he was sharply criticized by a Union governor who opposed the drafting of young men from his state. To explain to one of his military officers how he dealt with this governor, Lincoln told the story of a farmer whose field had a large log right in the middle of it. The farmer told his neighbors one Sunday that he had managed to get rid of the log. "How did you do it? It was too big to haul out, too knotty to split, and too wet and soggy to burn. What did you do?" the neighbors asked. The farmer replied, "Well, now boys, if you won't divulge the secret, I tell you how I got rid of it—**I plowed around** it." Lincoln concluded his tale: "Now, don't tell anybody, but that's the way I got rid of Governor ——, I plowed around him, but it took me three mortal hours to do it, and I was afraid every minute he'd see what I was at."[11]

Probably the most difficult decision that Lincoln had to make as president concerned slavery. Early in his tenure in office, Radical Republicans in Congress began to pressure Lincoln to emancipate the slaves as a proper response to the South's secession and its war to achieve independence. Through the first twenty months of the war, however, Lincoln offered the South the option of returning to the Union with slavery intact. Explaining his reticence to free the slaves early in 1862 to George Templeton Strong, an officer in the Sanitary Commission, which worked to improve the care of wounded soldiers, Lincoln told the story of three Methodist parsons traveling to Illinois. They knew that they would have to cross a stream before reaching their destination; they knew that the stream would be "ugly to cross, ye know, because the waters was up." As the three men rode, one parson suggested crossing the stream one way, and the second suggested another way. The third parson settled the argument, saying, "Brethren, this here talk ain't no use. I never cross a river until I come to it."[12] Lincoln issued the Emancipation Proclamation when he sensed that the moment was right, on January 1, 1863.

Environmental imagery also worked its way into Lincoln's speeches and writings, both formal and informal. One of his first important formal public addresses was delivered at the Young Men's Lyceum of Springfield, Illinois, on January 27, 1838. Lincoln was still somewhat new in town, having moved to Springfield less than a year earlier. But he was already well known, having served in the Illinois assembly and worked in Springfield as an attorney. Lincoln's subject was an important one: the perpetuation of Amreica's democratic political institutions. He opened his address by stating that his generation of Americans had inherited a good land governed by political institutions designed to safeguard citizens' civil and religious liberties. The nation was safe from foreign invasion, yet it was still in danger from "the increasing disregard for law which pervades the country; the growing disposition to substitute the wild and furious passions, in lieu of the sober judgment of Courts; and the worse than savage mobs, for the executive ministers of justice." He cited recent examples of mob justice in St. Louis and Mississippi. Lincoln offered a solution: "Let every American, every lover of liberty, every well wisher to his posterity, swear by the blood of the Revolution, never to violate in the least particular the laws of the country; and never to tolerate their violation by others."[13] The United States had endured for more than fifty years, but Lincoln saw new dangers arising from within the nation.

In the Young Men's Lyceum address, Lincoln used farm and nature metaphors to highlight the current threat to the American experiment in democratic government. The American Revolution generation had secured independence from Great Britain and set up a democratic government. "They succeeded. The experiment is successful; and thousands have won their deathless names in making it so. But the game is caught; and I believe it is true, that with the catching, end the pleasures of the chase. This field of glory is harvested, and the crop is already appropriated. But new reapers will arise, and *they*, too, will seek a field." Men of ambition will arise who are not satisfied with supporting and maintaining a government established by others. An American Alexander the Great, a Caesar, or a Napoleon will arise, a leader who will see no glory in maintaining the status quo; such a leader will look not to "tread in the footsteps of *any* predecessor, however illustrious," and that ambitious urge might threaten the democratic institutions of this new republic. Lincoln paid homage to the generation of the American Revolution. "But *those* histories are gone. . . . They are gone. They *were* a forest of giant oaks; but the all-resistless hurricane has swept over them, and left only, here and there, a lonely trunk, despoiled of its verdure, shorn of its foliage; unshading and unshaded, to murmur in a few more gentle breezes, and to combat with its mutilated limbs, a few more ruder storms, then to sink, and be no more." What the nation needs now to survive is the rule of reason: "Passion has helped us; but can do so no more.

It will in future be our enemy. Reason, cold, calculating unimpassioned reason, must furnish all the materials for our future support and defence."[14]

By 1850, slavery was emerging as the key political and moral issue that had absorbed—and was threatening—the nation. Antislavery politicians had opposed U.S. involvement in the Mexican War, fought from 1846 through 1848, in part because they believed that any territory gained during the conflict would eventually be carved into slave states. When the question of California's statehood arose in 1850, slavery again was part of the discussion. The debate over slavery continued in 1854, when Senator Stephen Douglas proposed the Kansas-Nebraska Act. In an 1858 speech, delivered when Lincoln was running against Douglas for an Illinois U.S. Senate seat, he claimed, "I have always hated slavery, I think as much as any Abolitionist."[15] An early expression of Lincoln's distaste for slavery appears in a letter that he wrote to Mary Speed, half-sister of his friend Joshua Speed, in September 1841. In the Speed letter, Lincoln wrote of a recent steamboat journey that he and Joshua had taken from Springfield, Illinois, to St. Louis. Lincoln described to Mary Speed a troubling scene that he had witnessed on the steamboat, "a fine example . . . for contemplating the effect of *condition* upon human happiness." A passenger on the boat had in his possession twelve slaves from Kentucky. "They were chained six and six together," wrote Lincoln, ". . . precisely like so many fish upon a trot-line. In this condition they were being separated forever from scenes of their childhood, their friends, their fathers and mothers, and brothers and sisters, and many of them, from their wives and children, and going into perpetual slavery where the lash of the master is proverbially more ruthless."[16]

Lincoln's comparison of the chained slaves and fish on a trot-line is telling. In their natural state of existence, the fish swim freely in their waters, but now they have been snared and held on a trot-line, never to be free again and to die in captivity. Lincoln made another analogy between slaves and creatures from the natural environment in an address that he delivered at a Sanitary Fair in Baltimore in 1864, while he served as president. In that address, Lincoln attempted a definition of the word *liberty*: "With some the word liberty may mean for each man to do as he pleases with himself, and the product of his labor; while with others the same word may mean for some men to do as they please with other men, and the product of other men's labor." He was clearly articulating the difference between slave owners and those against slavery—whether owning slaves was a basic right or living free was a basic right. To explain his point, Lincoln spoke of a shepherd, his sheep, and a wolf: "The shepherd drives the wolf from the sheep's throat, for which the sheep thanks the shepherd as a *liberator*, while the wolf denounces him for the same act as the destroyer of liberty, especially as the sheep was a black one." Lincoln's point was clear: "Plainly the sheep and the wolf are not agreed upon a definition of the word liberty; and precisely the same difference prevails to-day among us creatures, even in the North, and all professing to love liberty."[17]

The natural environment surely provided Lincoln with analogies and metaphors when he addressed the slavery issue. But perhaps the natural environment to which he was so closely connected during the first twenty-two years of his life did more than that; perhaps it had actually *shaped* in some ways Lincoln's views on human bondage. Fish swimming in a river and sheep grazing in a field lived freely; according to Lincoln, they had the right to be protected from the fisherman's trot-line and the wolf. Surely, if creatures like fish and sheep were entitled to live freely in their environment, human beings had a right to live freely in theirs. Hence, slavery was, for Lincoln, a violation of the natural order.

Lincoln first began to deal publicly with the slavery issue after the passage of the Kansas-Nebraska Act in 1854. The act's passage alarmed him and prompted his reentry into politics. The Missouri Compromise of 1820 had stipulated that slavery would be excluded from United States territories north of latitude 36°30'. The Kansas-Nebraska Act essentially nullified the Missouri Compromise by introducing the concept of popular sovereignty, proposed by Illinois senator Stephen Douglas. The residents of a territory, regardless of its location, could allow or outlaw slavery by a majority vote. In Lincoln's view, the Kansas-Nebraska Act threatened to extend slavery across the nation. He had long assumed that slavery, contained in the South, would eventually die. "In 1854, his profession had almost superseded the thought of politics to his mind," Lincoln wrote in his 1860 presidential campaign autobiography, "when the repeal of the Missouri compromise aroused him as he had never been before."[18] Lincoln began to make a series of speeches on slavery and the new legislation that he believed enabled it.

Lincoln used cattle and hogs to signal his opposition to the repeal of the Missouri Compromise. In September 1854, a few months after the passage of the Kansas-Nebraska Act, Lincoln engaged in a debate on the editorial pages of the *Illinois Journal* with John Calhoun, an Illinois Democratic Party leader who supported the act. Calhoun and other advocates of the Kansas-Nebraska Act claimed that the new law was not intended to spread slavery to new territories but merely to reorganize the Kansas-Nebraska territory and move it toward statehood. Lincoln disagreed. To make his point, Lincoln proposed the idea that he owned a farm with "a fine meadow, containing beautiful springs of water, and well fenced, which John Calhoun had agreed with Abraham (originally owning the land in common) should be his, and the agreement had been consummated in the most solemn manner, regarded by both as sacred." But Calhoun has acquired a large herd of cattle, and in time, his prairie grass has dried up, and there is no convenient body of water from which his cattle can drink. Calhoun knocks down the fences around Lincoln's meadow, allowing his cattle to graze and drink on Lincoln's land. Lincoln protests the removal of his fence, but Calhoun says, "I have taken down your fence; but nothing more. It is my true intent and meaning not to drive my cattle into your meadow, nor to exclude them therefrom, but to leave them perfectly free to form their own notions of the feed, and to direct their movements in their own way!"[19] Lincoln's point was clear: Once the barriers were removed from formerly free territory, slave owners would move in and occupy it.

Lincoln used the cattle analogy in his speech on the Kansas-Nebraska Act in Springfield a month later and again in a speech in Bloomington, Illinois, the following May. In another speech, he used hogs: "If I have a field . . . around which the cattle or hogs linger and crave to pass the fence, and I go and tear down the fence, will it be supposed that I do not by that act encourage them to enter? *Even the hogs would know better*—Much more *men*, who are a higher order of the animal world."[20] Lincoln likely wrote of hogs and cattle to appeal to rural citizens, a majority in central Illinois, who understood agriculture and the natural world. But during his own farming years, he had clearly learned lessons about land and animals that remained with him for many years, and those lessons took shape in his political rhetoric and informed his political positions.

During the Civil War, Lincoln, as president, often relied on nature analogies and metaphors to present military strategy. He frequently admitted to being an amateur regarding military tactics, because of his very limited military experience, so using examples from the natural environment to make a point was a way for him to make sense of complex military problems. For example, in a communication to Union general Joseph Hooker in June 1863, a month before the Battle of Gettysburg, Lincoln used an ox to suggest a strategy for Hooker's army. Confederate general Robert E. Lee was moving his troops north of the Rappahannock River in Virginia toward Pennsylvania, and General Hooker's army was keeping a close watch. Lincoln surmised that General Lee might leave a portion of his force in Fredericksburg, Virginia, on the other side of the Rappahannock, tempting General Hooker to attack that force. Lincoln warned Hooker against allowing the river to divide his troops: "In one word, I would not take any risk of being entangled upon the river, like an ox jumped half over a fence, and liable to be torn by dogs, front and rear, without a fair chance to gore one way or kick the other. If Lee would come to my side of the river, I would keep on the same side & fight him, or act on the defence." Writing again to General Hooker nine days later, Lincoln stated, "If the head of Lee's army is at Martinsburg [Virginia] and the tail of it on the Plank road between Fredericksburg and Chancellorsville, the animal must be very slim somewhere. Could you not break him?"[21]

Early in July 1863, General Lee's army clashed with Union troops at the Battle of Gettysburg, probably the most crucial battle of the entire war. The Confederates were defeated after three days of bitter fighting and retreated to Virginia. Lincoln extolled the Union victory at Gettysburg but was disappointed that General George Meade, the commander of Union troops during the battle, had not vigorously pursued Lee and destroyed his retreating army, an action that, in Lincoln's view, might have brought the war to a quick close. Writing to Union general Oliver Howard, Lincoln stated, "I was deeply mortified by the escape of Lee across the Potomac [River], because the substantial destruction of his army would have ended the war, and because I believed, such destruction was perfectly easy—believed that Gen. Meade and his noble army had expended all the skill, and toil, and blood, up to the ripe harvest, and then let the crop go to waste."[22]

By that time, the summer of 1863, Lincoln might have come to see the entire Civil War as one foul harvest. The conflict, which Lincoln had originally hoped would be limited in scope and swiftly decided, had caused tens of thousands of deaths and left much of the country a wasteland, both physically and spiritually. Lincoln articulated that idea in a brief address to some White House visitors from Missouri and Kansas in October 1863, three months after the horrific battle at Gettysburg:

> Actual war coming, blood grows hot, and blood is spilled. Thought is forced from old channels into confusion. Deception breeds and thrives. Confidence dies, and universal suspicion reigns. Each man feels an impulse to kill his neighbor, lest he be first killed by him. Revenge and retaliation follow. And all this, as before said, may be among honest men only. But this is not all. Every foul bird comes abroad, and every dirty reptile rises up. These add crime to confusion. Strong measures, deemed indispensable but harsh at best, such men make worse by maladministration. Murders for old grudges, and murders for pelf, proceed under any cloak that will best cover the occasion.[23]

The foul birds and reptiles to which Lincoln referred were fighters like Quantrill's Raiders, Southern guerrillas under the leadership of William Quantrill, who attacked Lawrence, Kansas, on August 21, 1863, burning the town and killing civilians, even children.

This statement is one of the most pessimistic in the entire Lincoln canon. The war had become catastrophic; "a mighty scourge of war,"

Lincoln later called it in his Second Inaugural Address.[24] The great American experiment in democracy was perhaps on its deathbed, suffering from self-inflicted wounds. Was any redemption in sight for the nation? During the month after he spoke so pessimistically to his visitors from Kansas and Missouri, Lincoln might have found some form of redemption, and he discovered it, perhaps, and later articulated it in the rhythms of the natural environment of his youth. The prompt was a letter from David Wills, on behalf of Governor Andrew Curtin of Pennsylvania, dated November 2, 1863. A cemetery was being established on the Gettysburg battlefield for those who had died there in combat, and Lincoln was invited "to be present, and participate in" a dedication ceremony on November 19. Specifically, Lincoln was invited to "formally set apart these grounds to their Sacred use by a few appropriate remarks," to be offered after the keynote oration, which would be delivered by the great orator Edward Everett.[25]

The Gettysburg Address is Lincoln's best-known, and to many his greatest, speech. It is short, 272 words, and was delivered in a few minutes' time. Lincoln's immediate task was to pay homage to the thousands of brave men who had perished in the battle, but Lincoln felt the need to go beyond that immediate goal. The war had dragged on for more than two and a half years. The death toll was in the hundreds of thousands; thousands of Union and Confederate soldiers had died on the Gettysburg battlefield four months earlier. Lincoln needed to articulate to his countrymen and countrywomen why the nation was enduring this national tragedy; he had to assign this terrible war, this foul harvest, a noble purpose in an attempt to give it some worthwhile meaning. The war, which had begun as a result of Southern secession, had become a war to abolish American slavery beginning on January 1, 1863.

Lincoln began by mentioning the birth of the nation: "Four score and seven years ago our fathers brought forth on this continent, a new nation, conceived in Liberty, and dedicated to the proposition that all men are created equal." But now "a great civil war" is "testing whether that nation, or any nation so conceived and dedicated, can long endure." The purpose of the day's event is "to dedicate a portion of that field, as a final resting place for those who here gave their lives that that nation might live," a "fitting and proper" endeavor. "The brave men, living and dead, who struggled here" had consecrated the Gettysburg battlefield, but it is the task of the living to remain dedicated to "the unfinished work which they who fought here have thus far so nobly advanced," to make certain that "these honored dead . . . shall not have died in vain" and that "this nation, under God, shall have a new birth of freedom—and that government of the people, by the people, for the people, shall not perish from the earth."[26]

Without specifically employing environmental imagery, Lincoln's short Gettysburg Address alludes to and moves with the rhythms of the natural world. Two prominent scholars who have devoted books to the speech, Gabor Boritt and Garry Wills, have identified that movement: "Birth, sacrificial death, rebirth. A born-again nation," states Boritt. Wills cites in the speech "the suggestive images of birth, testing, and rebirth."[27] The Founders gave birth to, "brought forth," a new nation "conceived in Liberty." But as this Civil War raged, the nation was going through a torturous near-death experience, personified by the many "honored dead" of Gettysburg. What possible good could come from such horrendous destruction and suffering? The nation, according to Lincoln, would experience "a new birth of freedom"; it would become a restored nation newly "dedicated to the proposition that all men are created equal." For the war to have meaning, it had to do more than merely reunite the fractured nation in some fragile postwar union and prove that democratic government can work; it would have to fundamentally change the nation for the better. The war would have to prompt the nation to expand Thomas Jefferson's assertion in the Declaration of Independence, the nation's founding document, that "all men are created equal" and entitled to "life, liberty, and the pursuit of happiness." Lincoln was comparing the nation to the flora of the natural environment. Seeds are planted in springtime; plants grow, flower, and bear fruit in the summer months; then they die when winter arrives. But new birth comes with the spring warmth and sunshine. If Lincoln's nation could have that experience, then the war's death and destruction, the buried soldiers at Gettysburg, would have some meaning. A national rebirth might follow the death and destruction of war and provide a new harvest for the nation.

Despite the destructive war that he and his nation waged, Lincoln had somehow remained psychologically connected to the rhythms of the natural world of his youth and young manhood. Perhaps his presidential lifestyle enabled him to do so. During his four years in office, Lincoln spent about 25 percent of his time away from the Executive Mansion at a summer White House, Soldiers' Home. He spent most evenings there from early summer through late autumn.[28] The home, located on a tree-shaded hill three miles north of the White House, was built by George W. Riggs, a wealthy Washingtonian, in 1842 on a plantation called Pleasant Hills. In 1850, Riggs sold the land, home, and outbuildings to the U.S. government, and it was used as a home for disabled veterans of the War of 1812. Lincoln's presidential predecessor, James Buchanan, had also used the home as a summer escape from the White House. At the time of the Civil War, the natural environment surrounding the White House was horrific, especially in summertime. A nearby soap factory gave off an offensive odor. The polluted Washington Canal, used as waste receptacle, flowed near the White House. The canal, originally designed to connect Washington to the Ohio River to accommodate trade, had fallen into disuse and become an essentially stagnant body of water, a breeding ground for insects and disease. The White House itself was insufferably hot and stuffy in the summer months.[29] In contrast, Soldiers' Home was, according to one newspaper account, "one of the most charming rural retreats in the vicinity of Washington."[30]

At Soldiers' Home, Lincoln escaped the heat and humidity of urban Washington and lived close to nature. Presidential business sometimes followed him there; he held meetings at Soldiers' Home and wrote speeches there. But Lincoln also traveled to Soldiers' Home after a day at his White House office to clear his mind, read, take walks, and breathe fresh air. Certainly the pleasant natural environment of Soldiers' Home helped Lincoln do all that and reconnected him spiritually to the natural environment of his youth. An episode recorded by Lincoln's White House secretary John Hay in his diary illustrates how the natural environment of Soldiers' Home might have soothed Lincoln. On the evening of August 23, 1863, Lincoln, Hay, and a woman whom Hay calls Mrs. Young visited the U.S. Naval Observatory, which had a powerful new telescope. "The Presdt. took a look at the moon & Arcturus [a star]," Hay wrote in his diary. "I went with him to the Soldiers' Home & he read Shakespeare to me, the end of Henry VI and the beginning of Richard III till my heavy eye-lids caught his considerate notice & he sent me to bed."[31] Visits to the observatory and evenings at Soldiers' Home kept Lincoln connected to the natural environment at a time when the nation was being torn asunder by war.

Another incident reveals that Lincoln's rural roots ran deep. One evening, Lincoln joined a group of women visiting Soldiers' Home. The women were admiring a stately tree on the premises. One woman claimed that the tree was a cedar, the other a spruce. Lincoln settled the debate. "Let me discourse on something I understand," Lincoln reportedly said. "I know all about trees in sight of being a backwoodsman. I'll show you the difference between spruce, pine, and cedar, and this shred of green, which is neither one nor the other but a kind of illegitimate cypress." Lincoln then gathered samples of each kind of tree and explained to the women the features of its foliage.[32]

Lincoln's great appetite for reading might also have kept him spiritually connected to the natural environment after he had physically departed from it. His reading was eclectic—histories, legal texts, works on science, works of humor, Shakespeare's plays—but he loved poetry as well. One of Lincoln's favorite authors was the British poet Lord George Gordon Byron, whose poems Lincoln likely began reading when he was in his twenties.[33] A favorite Byron poem was *Childe Harold's Pilgrimage*, a long narrative poem arranged in four cantos, written from 1812 through 1818. The poem depicts the journey through life of a melancholy young man named Harold, who finds momentary escape from his worldly problems in natural landscapes like the woods. Canto IV of Byron's poem reads:

Abraham Lincoln used Soldiers' Home as a summer White House, affording himself and his family an escape from the heat and humidity of urban Washington. Library of Congress.

> There is a pleasure in the pathless woods,
>   There is a rapture on the lonely shore,
>   There is society where none intrudes,
>   By the deep Sea, and Music in its roar:
>   I love not Man the less, but Nature more,
>   From these our interviews, in which I steal
>   From all I may be, or have been before,
>   To mingle with the Universe, and feel
>   What I can ne'er express—yet can not all conceal.[34]

Lincoln's evenings at Soldiers' Home might have done for him what the woods did for Byron's Harold.

He also cherished the work of the Massachusetts-born poet William Cullen Bryant, whom Lincoln came to know when Bryant emerged as an important political voice as editor of the *New-York*

Evening Post, whose editorial pages advocated abolition before and during the Civil War. Bryant's poems such as "To a Waterfowl," "A Forest Hymn," and "Inscription for the Entrance to a Wood," written between 1818 and 1824, as the nation was becoming more industrialized, extolled the virtues of retaining a connection with the natural environment. Lincoln committed to memory Bryant's long poem "Thanatopsis," a meditation on death.[35] Bryant was among the first New Yorkers to urge the creation of New York City's Central Park, which would offer city dwellers a temporary escape from urban life, proposing the park in an editorial in the *New-York Evening Post* on the eve of July 4, 1844. Bryant's editorial lamented that New Yorkers had no open space to celebrate Independence Day.[36] Bryant's forty-two-line "Inscription for the Entrance to a Wood" opens with an invitation:

> Stranger, if thou hast learned a truth which needs
> No school of long experience, that the world
> Is full of guilt and misery, and hast seen
> Enough of all its sorrows, crimes, and cares,
> To tire thee of it, enter this wild wood
> And view the haunts of nature. The calm shade
> Shall bring a kindred calm, and the sweet breeze
> That makes the green leaves dance, shall waft a balm
> To thy sick heart. Thou wilt find nothing here
> Of all that pained thee in the haunts of men,
> And made thee loathe thy life. [37]

If Lincoln did not take frequent walks in the woods, he at least remained vicariously connected to the woods and the natural environment by reading Bryant's poems.

Lincoln also enjoyed reading travel narratives that connected him spiritually to the wild and unpopulated sections of the country. He read John Frémont's 1845 *Report of the Exploring Expedition to the Rocky Mountains*, J. Quinn Thornton's *Oregon and California in 1848*, Baldwin Möllhausen's 1858 *Diary of a Journey from the Mississippi to the Coasts of the Pacific*, and Francis Parkman's *The Oregon Trail*, published in 1849.[38] Parkman's narrative, an account of a two-month excursion that he took through the Rocky Mountains in the summer of 1846, vividly captured the stark beauty of the uncivilized sections of the American West, a region that Lincoln never visited. In one section of his text, Parkman captures the beauty and dignity of Colorado's Pikes Peak:

> We encamped among ravines and hollows, through which a little brook was foaming angrily. Before sunrise in the morning the snow-covered mountains were beautifully tinged with a delicate rose-color. A noble spectacle awaited us as we moved forward. Six or eight miles to our right, Pike's Peak and his giant brethren rose out of the level prairie, as if springing from the bed of the ocean. From their summits down to the plain below they were involved in a mantle of clouds, in restless motion, as if urged by strong winds.[39]

With a book in his hand, Lincoln could vicariously travel to places of natural beauty like Pikes Peak and keep the natural environment in his mind.

Three symbols have remained closely attached to Abraham Lincoln: the log cabin, the ax, and the top hat. The top hat, an article of formal wear donned by mid-nineteenth-century gentlemen of fashion, represents Lincoln's life as a successful lawyer and politician. The log cabin and ax represent Lincoln's rural upbringing, his early life in the natural environment. Both lives were part of Lincoln's identity. In his landmark essay *Nature*, published in 1836, the American transcendentalist philosopher Ralph Waldo Emerson envisioned a man who might hold such a dual identity: "We know more from nature than we can at will communicate. Its light flows into the mind evermore, and we forget its presence. The poet, the orator, bred in the woods, whose senses have been nourished by their fair and appeasing changes, year after year, without design and without heed,—shall not lose their lesson altogether, in the roar of cities or the broil of politics." Even "amidst agitation and terror in national councils,—in the hour of revolution," images of nature "shall reappear in their morning lustre. . . . At the call of a noble sentiment, again the woods wave, the pines murmur, the river rolls and shines, and the cattle low upon the mountains, as he saw and heard them in his infancy."[40] Lincoln might not have read *Nature* (though he did read other Emerson essays),[41] but perhaps he personifies Emerson's abstract orator bred in the woods who calls upon the woods, rivers, and farm animals of his infancy for inspiration in the "broil of politics" and the "hour of revolution." Throughout his life, Lincoln would continue to see in his mind his rural childhood home and its surrounding natural environment, which would shape him, his outlook, and his rhetoric in profound ways.

THIS MIGHTY SCOURGE OF WAR

An environmental biography of Abraham Lincoln must include a chapter on the major event of his lifetime, the Civil War. When he took office as president on March 4, 1861, however, Lincoln was surely not expecting to wage the most devastating war in U.S. history, one that would cause more than seven hundred thousand deaths, result in great political and economic upheaval, and incur widespread infrastructure and environmental damage. The slavery debate had dangerously divided the nation for more than a decade, and blood had been shed over slavery in "Bleeding Kansas" after the passage of the Kansas-Nebraska Act in 1854 and at Harpers Ferry, Virginia, during John Brown's failed attempt to raid a federal arsenal and arm slaves on nearby plantations in 1859. But before the election of 1860, the political leaders of neither the North nor the South were calling for a civil war to resolve the issue, and talk of Southern secession was not widespread. Lincoln did not anticipate that his presidency would be dominated by a great civil war that would last four years—his entire tenure in office—and result in the abolition of American slavery. The warning signs of such a war were apparent in the weeks following the 1860 election, but Lincoln optimistically hoped that an armed conflict over slavery, and its accompanying carnage, could be avoided.

From the time of his election on November 6, 1860, until the commencement of his presidency four months later, Lincoln played down the tensions between the North and the South caused by his election.

Two weeks after Election Day, he told a crowd of well-wishers gathered at his Springfield, Illinois, home, "Let us at all times remember that all American citizens are brothers of a common country, and should dwell together in the bonds of fraternal feeling." In February 1861, at a train stop in Pittsburgh on his way to Washington for his March 4 inauguration, Lincoln spoke to a crowd gathered at the train station: "My advice . . . is to keep cool. If the great American people will only keep their temper, on both sides of the line, the troubles will come to an end." In an address at Independence Hall in Philadelphia a week later, Lincoln said to his audience, "Now in my view of the present aspect of affairs, there is no need of bloodshed and war. There is no necessity for it." That same day, in a speech in Harrisburg to Governor Andrew J. Curtin of Pennsylvania and his state's militia, Lincoln expressed his hope that "in the shedding of blood their [the militia's] services may never be needed, especially in the shedding of fraternal blood."[1] But in the months before his inauguration, Lincoln told his fellow Republicans that he would remain firm in his decision not to compromise on his major campaign promise: to prohibit the expansion of slavery into new states and territories.

Many Southerners, fearful that a Republican president would advance the cause of abolition, were not committed to a peaceful resolution of their differences with the North. In December, South Carolina voted to secede from the Union, and over the next four months, ten other Southern states followed South Carolina's lead. Many Northerners viewed any attempt at secession as an act of civil war. A peace convention held in Washington a month before Lincoln's inauguration, headed by former president John Tyler, failed, mainly because not one of the seceded states had sent delegates to the convention. The states that had voted to secede from the Union were strongly committed to achieving their independence and were preparing for war if Lincoln did not acquiesce to their actions.

Lincoln's First Inaugural Address, delivered on March 4, 1861, was a plea for peace. He announced that there would be no bloodshed, no invasion of the South. He asserted that the Union "is perpetual, confirmed by the history of the Union itself," and that secession is anarchy. He promised to enforce the Fugitive Slave Law, so sharply criticized by abolitionists, and suggested that a recently proposed amendment to the Constitution prohibiting federal government interference with slavery in the states where it existed merited serious discussion. Lincoln closed his address with a rhetorical flourish, telling the South, "We are not enemies, but friends. We must not be enemies"; he optimistically predicted that the nation's "mystic chords of memory . . . will yet swell the chorus of the Union, when again touched, as surely they will be, by the better angels of our nature."[2]

But the war came. On April 12, Confederate troops fired on Fort Sumter off the coast of South Carolina after Lincoln had refused a demand to evacuate the fortress. Three days later, Lincoln issued a call for seventy-five thousand troops to put down the Southern rebellion. He ordered a blockade of Southern ports, designed to prevent the export of Southern cotton and other goods, seriously harming the South's economy. The South viewed the blockade as an act of war. On July 4, 1861, sensing that the Southern rebellion would not be temporary and that extensive military action would be necessary to end it, Lincoln sent a message to Congress, gathered in a special session called to deal with the Southern rebellion. He requested four hundred thousand new troops and $400 million to give him "the legal means for making this contest a short, and a decisive one."[3] Lincoln's assertion that the war could be short and decisive was consistent with what Northern generals believed.[4] Secretary of State William Seward optimistically told other members of Lincoln's cabinet that the war would be over in thirty days.[5] The North's press called for a quick victory. "Forward to Richmond!" the headlines of Northern newspapers screamed.[6] In his postwar memoirs, General William T. Sherman stated that while Northerners were calling for an invasion of Richmond and a quick and decisive end to the war, "Our Men had been told so often at home that all they had to do was make a bold appearance, and the rebels would run."[7] The short war that Lincoln and other Northerners envisioned would not result in a high number of casualties or cause great damage to cities, infrastructure, plantations and farmlands, or the natural landscape.

The Union's invasion of the South, its march to Richmond, which commenced in mid-July 1861, ended in a bitter defeat at the Battle of Bull Run. As Union troops limped back to Washington after the battle, Lincoln and his generals began to sense that the war to defeat the South's rebellion might take much longer than he had anticipated. But if the war would not be quick and decisive, it could at least be limited—confined to action on battlefields, sparing the nation great damage to farms and plantations, cities and towns, infrastructure, and the natural environment. Many of the Union and Confederate military leaders were West Point graduates: George McClellan, Philip Sheridan, Ambrose Burnside, George Meade, Ulysses S. Grant, Joseph Hooker, and William T. Sherman for the North; and P. G. T. Beauregard, Robert E. Lee, Jubal Early, and James Longstreet for the South. In the decades before the Civil War, cadets at West Point learned the art of war. This oxymoronic term described conflicts whose carnage was mainly limited to battlefields. Unlike ancient wars, these modern wars would feature a clash between armies on clearly defined battlefields and would not result in the slaughter of innocent civilians, the sacking of cities, and the destruction of natural landscapes. Widely used in war tactics courses at West Point in the decade before the Civil War was an 1846 text authored by Henry Halleck, a veteran of the Mexican War and later a Union General, titled *Elements of Military Art and Science.*[8] Lincoln, too, had read Halleck's volume.[9]

Even after the Battle of Bull Run had dashed Lincoln's hope for a short and decisive war, he still hoped to wage a limited war. Lincoln judged that many Southerners opposed the rebellion. He also believed that the country would eventually be reunited, and he did not want to wage a war of mass destruction against people who he believed were his fellow citizens and would soon be part of a reunited nation. Moreover, a harsh war might even stiffen Southern resistance, prolonging the conflict. Two of Lincoln's key Union generals early in the war, Don Carlos Buell and George McClellan, believed that the war should be conducted humanely according to the scientific principles set down in military tactics textbooks such as Halleck's. Armies could advance into Southern territories and occupy them without firing too many shots. Armies would keep the peace rather than wage war. When armies did wage war, the action would be confined to the battlefield and not cause great damage to cities and natural landscapes.[10] In July 1862, a year into the war, McClellan sent Lincoln a lengthy letter detailing his notion of a limited war. The war, according to McClellan, "should be conducted upon the highest known Christian principles." Its goal should not be "the subjugation of the people of any state"; private property should not be confiscated or destroyed; "pillage and waste should be treated as high crimes." McClellan believed that the Union's armies "should be mainly collected into masses and brought upon the armies of the Confederate States; and those armies thoroughly defeated, the political structure which they support would soon cease to exist."[11]

At that point in the war, General Sherman agreed with McClellan. On September 21, 1862, he wrote in a letter to the editor of the *Memphis Bulletin*, published in rebellious Tennessee, where his army was stationed, "I admit the law to be that no officer or soldier of the United States shall commit waste or destruction of cornfields, orchards, potato-patches, or any kind of pillage on friend or foe near Memphis, and that I stand prepared to execute the law as far as possible."[12] In this letter, Sherman was specifically prohibiting his troops from causing damage to the South's natural landscapes. He regularly had the rules of war read to his troops. He once placed one of his captains under military arrest for ordering the burning of a cotton gin in a Southern state. Looking back at that early part of the war, Sherman later wrote, "I, poor innocent, would not let a soldier take a green apple or a fence rail to make a cup of coffee."[13]

But the North's limited-war strategy was not accomplishing Lincoln's goal of quickly subduing the South's rebellion and reestablishing the Union. For the first eighteen months of the conflict, armies clashed, soldiers died in great numbers, and the nation was still divided. The South was not giving up, as Lincoln had originally hoped. For the North, the war was, at best, a stalemate, and Lincoln began to fear that Northerners, tired of war and sick from reading the lists of the dead soldiers in their local newspapers, would demand peace in exchange for Southern independence. From the commencement of combat, however, some Northerners, mainly Republicans, had called for a more aggressive war plan for the North. Some had advocated the burning of Montgomery, Alabama, the first Confederate capital (before Richmond). Even before Lincoln took office, Republican senator Benjamin Wade of Ohio, reacting to the first votes of secession, called for "making the south a desert."[14] At the start of the war, Confederate president Jefferson Davis swore that his armies would destroy Northern cities if the South were not granted independence.[15]

Events that took place in September 1862, eighteen months after Lincoln had assumed the presidency, signaled an end to the limited war that the North had been waging. General Lee had commenced an invasion of the North, marching his Army of Northern Virginia into Maryland, but on September 17, his army was stopped in the bloody Battle of Antietam near Sharpsburg by General McClellan's Army of the Potomac. More than six thousand Union and Confederate soldiers died of wounds suffered that day,[16] dispelling any lingering notions that this civil war could be limited. After the battle, Lee retreated to Virginia, and Lincoln urged McClellan to pursue Lee and destroy his army, a move that Lincoln reasoned might end the war. McClellan balked, claiming that his army needed rest. Lincoln then sacked McClellan, a main proponent of the limited-war strategy. On September 22, Lincoln issued his Preliminary Emancipation Proclamation, announcing that on January 1, 1863, he would issue a proclamation freeing all slaves in the states in rebellion. The stakes of the war were now significantly raised. A few Northern battlefield victories, followed by intense negotiations and compromises on the slavery issue, would not end the rebellion. At stake for the South were its economy and its way of life, both of which relied on slavery as a foundation. The South would have to be conquered and subdued, and a more aggressive war strategy would be necessary to accomplish the North's goal. Lincoln made good on his September promise; he issued the Emancipation Proclamation on January 1, 1863.

Three key Union generals stood ready to implement the North's new, more aggressive war policy: Ulysses S. Grant, William T. Sherman, and Philip Sheridan. In the summer of 1862, before the Battle of Antietam, Grant had been calling for a more aggressive war, a war of complete conquest that would ruin the South's agricultural landscape and economy. Destroying Southern plantations, the symbol of the

South's identity and prosperity, would signal to its population that its cause would be lost.[17] Lincoln gradually came around to Grant's point of view. Lincoln appointed Grant general in chief of the Union army in March 1864, but even before then, Grant, Sherman, and other Union generals had been carrying out the more aggressive strategy, which would cause great damage to the South's infrastructure and natural landscape. In their summer 1863 Mississippi campaign, which culminated in a July victory at the Battle of Vicksburg, Generals Grant and Sherman were raiding plantations, killing or confiscating livestock, and confiscating produce. After Vicksburg fell, Sherman boasted that "the land is devastated for thirty miles around."[18] The gentler war that McClellan had recommended to Lincoln in the summer of 1862 had given way to a total war to devastate the South.

Perhaps Sherman, more than any other Union general, personified the North's concept of total war. Early in the war, he had attempted to respect civilians and civilian property. But during his military campaigns, he often faced guerrilla fighters, nonuniformed Southern citizens who attacked his army. In August 1862, Sherman had written to Treasury Secretary Salmon Chase that "the government of the United States may now safely proceed on the proper rule that all in the South are enemies of all in the North." A month later, Sherman wrote to Horatio Wright, a newspaper correspondent, "The people of the South are now on duty as soldiers."[19] Hence, in Sherman's view, the people of the South, not just its armies, should feel the pain of war. Their cities, towns, and landscapes would have to suffer to force the rebellious South to surrender. Sherman's military masterpieces were his conquest of Atlanta, Georgia, in the late summer of 1864 and his subsequent March to the Sea. On the way to Atlanta, his troops tore up railroad tracks, cut telegraph wires, and destroyed bridges. Writing in his memoirs about the destruction that his army wrought in Georgia, Sherman stated, "If the people raise a howl against my barbarity and cruelty, I will answer that war is war, and not popularity-seeking. If they want peace, they and their relatives must stop the war." Sherman's troops laid siege to Atlanta, firing shells into the city and destroying buildings. Writing to the mayor and councilmen of Atlanta before he ordered an evacuation of the city, Sherman asserted, "You cannot qualify war in harsher terms than I will. War is cruelty, and you cannot refine it; and those who brought war into our country deserve all the curses and malediction a people can pour out."[20] After civilians evacuated Atlanta, Sherman ordered large sections of the city burned.

Lincoln was very aware of the way Sherman was waging war. The president visited the War Department daily, anxiously reading any messages regarding the war that came across the telegraph cables. Sherman kept Lincoln informed of his tactics, and Lincoln chose not to restrict Sherman in any way. By the time of Sherman's assault on

General William T. Sherman, with President Lincoln's approval, committed his troops to a total war against the Confederacy. Library of Congress.

Atlanta, Lincoln had accepted the idea that a more aggressive and destructive war would be necessary to break the South's resistance.[21] But the war took a personal toll on Lincoln. He sadly watched as Washington military hospitals filled up with the wounded, whom he regularly visited. One Lincoln scholar who has studied his final months describes him as "care worn and haggard" as the war casualties mounted.[22] In a conversation with Indiana congressman Daniel Voorhees late in the war, Lincoln rhetorically asked, "Doesn't it strike you as queer that I, who couldn't cut the head off a chicken, and was sick at the sight of blood, should be cast into the middle of a great war, with blood flowing all about me?"[23] Nonetheless, the bleeding and the destruction continued, with Lincoln's approval.

Sherman occupied Atlanta from early September through mid-November 1864, then commenced his famous March to the Sea. "Behind us lay Atlanta, smoldering in ruins, the black smoke rising high in the air, and hanging like a pall over the ruined city," Sherman wrote in his memoirs about his departure from Atlanta. Writing to Grant about his planned march through Georgia, Sherman, the general who early in the war had punished soldiers who damaged civilian properties, stated that "the utter destruction of its roads, houses, and people will cripple their [the Confederates'] military resources. . . . I can make this march, and make Georgia howl!" Sherman proposed that his army would move through Georgia, "smashing things to the sea."[24] His army marched on Savannah, on the Georgia coast, then continued its scorched-earth tactics into South Carolina, the birthplace of secession. His soldiers torched the city of Columbia, burning the state house, schools, homes, hotels, and businesses. Although Sherman tried to limit the burning and pillaging, to the residents of Columbia who condemned him for his army's actions, Sherman flatly stated, "Such is the fortune of war."[25]

General Sheridan's venue was the Shenandoah Valley, a region noted for its great natural beauty. In the fall of 1864, while Sherman smashed things to the sea, Sheridan's troops ravished the valley. Following Grant's orders, Sheridan, too, had arrived at the conclusion that the South's rebellion could be subdued only if its entire population felt the hard hand of total war. "I do not hold war to mean simply that lines of men shall engage each other in battle, and material interests be ignored," he explained in his postwar memoirs. "This is but a duel, in which one combatant seeks the other's life; war means much more, and is far worse than this." In a letter to Grant penned in early October, Sheridan described the extensive damage that his army was inflicting on the Shenandoah countryside: "I have destroyed over 2,000 barns filled with wheat, hay and farming implements; over seventy mills filled with flour and wheat; have driven in front of the army over 4,000 head of stock, and have killed and issued to the troops not less than 3.000 sheep."[26] Sheridan's letter to Grant highlights a total war strategy repeated throughout the South. Union armies that moved through a Southern town or city often torched warehouses and barns that held bales of cotton or other supplies that might be of use to Confederate soldiers or even citizens.

In the hands of Grant, Sherman, and Sheridan, the North's leading generals, the Civil War had ceased to be the limited war that Lincoln had originally planned; it had become a total war. Given the breadth of the destruction, the weaponry, and the tactics, historians have labeled the Civil War as America's first modern war, anticipating the terrible European wars of the twentieth century. Lincoln, who had hoped for no war, then for a short and decisive war, and then for a limited war, privately and publicly endorsed his leading generals' belief that a total war would be necessary to end the South's rebellion and restore the Union. On September 3, the day after Atlanta fell to Union armies, Lincoln wrote to General Sherman congratulating and thanking him for his conquest of Atlanta: "The marches, battles, sieges, and other military operations that have signalized this campaign must render it famous in the annals of war, and have entitled those who have participated therein to the applause and thanks of the nation." That same day, Lincoln offered to the nation a public "Proclamation of Thanksgiving and Prayer" that praised "the glorious achievements of the Army under Major General Sherman in the State of Georgia, resulting in the capture of the City of Atlanta." On December 26, 1864, Lincoln wrote to Sherman praising him for his March to the Sea. Lincoln had initially been skeptical about Sherman's proposed march. "Now, the undertaking being a success, the honor is all yours," Lincoln wrote. The day before, Sherman had written to Lincoln, "I beg to present you as a Christmas gift the city of Savannah [Georgia] with 150 heavy guns & plenty of ammunition & also about 25000 bales of cotton." On March 3, 1865, the day before his second inauguration, Lincoln stated to a crowd of supporters gathered outside the White House, "Sherman went in at Atlanta and came out right. He has gone in again at Savannah, and I propose three cheers for his coming out gloriously."[27]

Lincoln realized that Union victories in Atlanta and in the Shenandoah Valley in the summer and fall of 1864 had helped get him re-elected in the presidential election of 1864. With the tide of the war finally flowing in the North's favor, Lincoln had soundly defeated the Democratic peace and anti-emancipation candidate, former general George McClellan.

The North was essentially spared the wrath of total war, though slave states loyal to the Union, such as Maryland and Kentucky, did incur serious damage. Most major battles and troop movements occurred in the South. The North's towns and cities, infrastructure, and natural landscape escaped the major carnage that occurred throughout much of the South, but the residents of Chambersburg, Pennsylvania, a town just north of the Virginia state line, felt war's hard hand on July 30, 1864, when Confederate general John McCausland's troops attacked and then burned the city, destroying 559 buildings, including homes, businesses, and barns.[28] Confederate general Jubal Early's raid on Washington in the summer of 1864 also caused damage to landscapes and property in Maryland.

The Civil War ended in the spring of 1865. The nation was reunited in a slave-free Union. But this total war had cost the nation dearly. In his Second Inaugural Address, delivered on March 4, 1865, about a month before the war ended, Lincoln called the conflict "this mighty scourge of war," comparing it to an instrument of torture. Lincoln had not anticipated such a long and devastating war when he delivered his First Inaugural Address four years earlier. "Neither party expected for the war, the magnitude, or the duration, which it has already attained," he stated in his Second Inaugural.[29] More than seven hundred thousand men died in combat or as a result of war wounds or diseases contracted during military service. Thousands of other men who fought returned home with limbs missing and other debilitating war wounds. The North had been spared the brunt of the battle, but the "mighty scourge of war" was evident throughout the South. The destruction included substantial environmental damage. Twenty-first-century environmental historians have called the Civil War "an environmental watershed for the nation," "an environmental catastrophe of the first magnitude, with effects that endured long after the guns were silenced," and "an ecological disaster."[30]

These historians have suggested that the Civil War even had an environmental cause. As cotton became the South's main cash crop, woodlands were cleared to make room for more cotton fields. When soils in the South became nutritionally depleted after several years of cotton planting with little attempt at crop rotation, new land had to be acquired to maintain the level of cotton production. Cotton farmers needed to migrate westward and acquire fresh territories for their cash crop, and they wanted to bring slave labor into those new territories.[31] Cotton production was also an important part of the South's identity. Lincoln's Republican Party was born in 1854, after the passage of the Kansas-Nebraska Act made possible the expansion of slavery into new territories. Lincoln and the Republicans pledged themselves, minimally, to limit the spread of slavery, and many Republicans were strongly abolitionist. Lincoln's election in 1860 spelled danger for the South's cotton planters and farmers, and they were willing to divide the nation and go to war to acquire new lands and fresh soil for their cash crop and their slaves.

Deforestation, a century-old problem, especially on the East Coast, was perhaps the most visible environmental effect of the Civil War. Civil War armies, consisting of tens of thousands of men marching hundreds of miles through the countryside, devoured wood. Both Union and Confederate armies included pioneer corps, soldiers who chopped down trees to create roads that enabled troop movement. When the track was too muddy for marching men and wagons, the pioneer corps created corduroy roads, trees laid side by side over which the troops traveled. Soldiers used wood to fuel fires for cooking and warmth, to construct fortifications and signal towers, to assemble structures to block pursuing enemy armies, to erect bridges over waterways, to build shelters in their camps. During the war, many Southern forests were reduced to stumps. By the end of the war, Richmond had no surrounding woodlands to supply residents with heating and building materials.[32] On Sherman's March to Sea, his army carved a path through the natural landscape sixty miles wide; in his Carolina campaign, his troops created four hundred miles of corduroy roads.[33]

Trees were damaged and destroyed during combat. Troops often used trees for cover. Cannonballs, shells, and even bullets from rifles damaged trees. One Massachusetts soldier marching through Virginia noticed the shots that trees had absorbed during a recent battle. Writing home to his mother about the experience, the soldier reported that "the bushes and trees here were completely riddled with bullets, there wasn't a twig the size of your finger that wasn't cut off, and trees the size of a man's body had, every one at least three or four bullets in it."[34] Daniel M. Holt, a Union surgeon who witnessed the Battle of Spotsylvania Court House in Virginia in 1864, wrote afterward, "Trees are perfectly riddled with bullets."[35] After another Virginia battle in 1865, Elijah Hunt Rhodes of the 2nd Rhode Island Infantry wrote in his diary, "The trees are splintered by shot and shell, and in one tree I counted sixteen bullets."[36] One of the early historians of the Civil War, Henry W. Elson, while researching his 1912 book, *The Civil War through the Camera*, came across an uncredited photograph taken of the forest after the Battle of the Wilderness, fought in the woodlands of Virginia in May 1864. The photo showed the great damage inflicted on trees by shot and shell during the battle. Elson appropriately titled his photographic find "Trees in the Track of an Iron Storm."[37] Exploding shells also caused forest fires. Near the end of the war, Frederick Starr Jr., working for the Department of Agriculture, wrote a report titled "American Forests: Their Destruction and Preservation," which stated that "the destruction of forests and timber during the war of rebellion has been immense."[38] One twenty-first-century environmental historian studying the Civil War estimates that two million of the South's trees were used during the war for construction and another twenty-five thousand died from war wounds.[39]

A battlefield near Peach Tree Creek in Georgia reveals the damage done to the natural landscape during the Civil War as Sherman's Union troops marched through Georgia. Library of Congress.

Trees were not the only environmental victims of the Civil War. When the North's generals, with Lincoln's wholehearted support, began to engage in total war, their armies trampled, looted, and burned plantations and farms. Green landscapes were turned into environmental wastelands. Wildlife and farm animals perished in the conflict. One study estimated that more than one million horses and mules lost their lives in combat. Another suggested that the hog population in war zones in Virginia and the Carolinas fell by 50 percent during the war.[40] The carcasses of animals littered the landscape after a battle, attracting insects and vermin. With their natural forest habitats severely reduced or completely destroyed, bird populations dropped.

Soils were poisoned by lead. A million or more bullets, shells, and cannonballs might be fired during a major battle, most of which entered the soil and remained there. In his memoirs, General Sherman wrote of ripping apart railroad tracks as his armies marched across the South. To prevent the tracks from being quickly reassembled, Sherman's troops would heat the iron rails, then twist them around trees or telegraph poles. The twisted rails, which became known as "Sherman's neckties," littered the Southern natural landscape wherever Sherman's armies marched.[41] Crops grown in lead-poisoned soils and animals that feed on lead-poisoned grasses can pass lead poisoning to humans, which can result in muscle and abdominal pain, tremors, memory loss, and kidney failure.

Sitting and moving armies caused water pollution. Armies often camped along rivers and streams. The waterways became latrines, the troops poisoning the water and creating a watery climate where bacteria and viruses thrived, leading to diseases such as dysentery and typhoid fever. Men crowded together in army camps spread diseases among themselves. During the Civil War, for every soldier who died in battle, two died of disease.[42] Tragically, one victim of the water pollution caused by a standing army was Lincoln's eleven-year-old son, Willie. The large Union army that Lincoln assembled at the beginning of the war to defend Washington against a Confederate attack from Virginia camped along the Potomac River. Water from that river was piped into the White House unfiltered. Early in 1862, both Willie and his older brother, Tad, became sick with fever. Tad recovered, but Willie died on February 20. He had contracted typhoid fever, a viral infection, often fatal in the nineteenth century, caused by contact with water polluted by human and animal feces.[43]

Lincoln, stationed in Washington, did not witness firsthand the extensive environmental devastation endured by the South during the Civil War. He did, however, visit Gettysburg to deliver his address four months after the great battle, and he visited Grant's army near Petersburg in 1865. In the immediate aftermath of the Battle of Gettysburg, the town was an environmental disaster area. The corpses of thousands of human beings and animals littered its fields. In the July heat, bluebottle flies and vultures descended on the battlefield. The stench was suffocating. Dead bodies, hurriedly buried in shallow graves in the days immediately after the battle, poked through the ground weeks later when rains washed the soil away. When Lincoln arrived in November to attend the cemetery dedication ceremony and deliver his Gettysburg Address, the burial of dead bodies was not yet completed, and the fields retained the scars of the battle.[44] So perhaps from surveying the Gettysburg battlefield, Lincoln got a sense of the damage wrought to the South's natural landscape during the four years of war. The South's landscape had endured many devastating battles like the one fought at Gettysburg. The natural landscape surrounding Petersburg, Virginia, which Lincoln witnessed on his visit, had also suffered extensive damage after a long, nine-month siege.

The environmental damage wrought by the Civil War could have been much worse. Early in the war, Lincoln received a letter from Samuel Small, a Canadian. Small had gotten news of "the much Lamented Rupture between Different States of our neighboring republic" and "felt much Incensed at the conduct of your S-Carolina and other south states Legislatures" that had voted for secession. Small offered Lincoln a way of quickly forcing the seceded states back into the Union: "War between the Contending Parties seems inevitable [so] I hereby transmit to you What for twelve years kept a secret from the World To Wit an Invention by which I can take one thousand cavalry and reduce the Whole South Territory to complete submission in three months." Small's suggestion was "to shock by the power of mercury any Army or Fleet that may be brought together Into a State of stupefaction so that They can easily be made Prisoners Bound and Secured without doing any material Injury." Small claimed that he had "tried it on Animals such as Bears Deer &c With full effect."[45] Using mercury gas or mercury-based weapons would have created serious and long-lasting environmental problems. Its presence in large quantities poisons air, soil, and water, which in turn poisons the food chain. Mercury poisoning in humans can result in a variety of skin and muscular ailments. Lincoln might not have seen Small's letter—he made no response. The letter might have been reviewed by Lincoln's War Department, which fortunately did not act on Small's proposal.

In May 1862, John W. Doughty, a New York schoolteacher, sent Lincoln a letter containing a design for a shell filled with chlorine gas "to be used for routing an entrenched enemy." Doughty explained that chlorine gas "diffused in the atmosphere produces uncontrollably violent coughing. A full inspiration would be fatal." If a shell containing chlorine gas were exploded over a fort or entrenchment, "the gas would by its great specific gravity, rapidly descend to the ground. The men could not dodge it, and their first intimation of its presence, would be by its inhalation, which would most effectually disqualify every man for service that was within the circle of its influence."[46] Such a weapon not only would have resulted in a miserable death for the soldiers who came in contact with it, but it also would have poisoned the natural landscape in which it was used for years to come, becoming part of the human food chain and causing cancers and other serious illnesses. Lincoln's War Department also—and wisely—chose not to act on Doughty's suggestion. Doughty wrote again two years later about his weapon, but again his proposal was ignored. A very similar weapon was used half a century later by the Germans against British and French troops during World War I, with horrific results.[47]

Other proposals for chemical weapons were advanced during the Civil War. Early in the conflict, Joseph Jones, a Confederate surgeon, developed designs for an artillery shell that would release phosphorus and hydrogen cyanide, a toxic gas. A correspondent for a Richmond, Virginia, newspaper proposed a shell containing alkarsin that would explode, causing an intense flame and the release of a poisonous gas. Other proposals included weapons containing arsenic, cayenne pepper, and nitic, sulfuric, and hydrochloric acids.[48] The use of such chemical weapons during the Civil War, which was fought at a time when the long-term effects of chemicals on ecosystems and human health were mostly unknown, could have had horrific environmental effects, poisoning natural landscapes for decades.

The environmental legacy of the Civil War continued after the fighting had ceased. Southern cities, towns, and railroads destroyed during the war had to be rebuilt. The forests of northern Georgia were chopped down to rebuild Atlanta, large portions of which had been burned by General Sherman's troops.[49] After the war, some regions of the South resembled wastelands, with tree stumps as the only sign of life. With their slaves liberated, many plantation owners could no longer maintain their acres of cotton, tobacco, and other crops, which over time went to weed. Many owners of small Southern farms died in the fighting, leaving no one to run their farms. Abandoned farmland did not quickly heal itself; it became impoverished.[50] The debris of war—wrecked wagons, disabled cannons, the rotting corpses of animals—littered Southern landscapes. After the war, Ambrose Bierce, who had fought for the Union army in major battles at Shiloh, Stones River, and Missionary Ridge, wrote more than two dozen short stories based on his wartime experiences. In one story, "Three and One Are One," a Union soldier, Barr Lassiter, pays a visit to his parents' home in rural Tennessee when his regiment is moving through the area. En route, he encounters a boyhood friend who ominously tells him, "There have been changes." When he reaches his home, Lassiter sees, where his family's home once stood, only "fire-blackened foundations of stone, enclosing an area of compact ashes pitted by rains."[51] Many Confederate soldiers returned from war to similar Southern wastelands and in poverty, which resulted in further environmental depletion.

The environmental damage incurred by the South also crippled its economy. After the war, sharecropping replaced slave labor, and agricultural production eventually improved to prewar levels, but the South remained economically challenged for more than half a century after the war ended.[52] In his 1929 novel, *The Sound and the Fury*, Mississippi author William Faulkner used the Compson family to personify the defeated South. Sixty years after the Civil War, the Compsons, once a wealthy and prominent Mississippi clan that boasted an antebellum governor and a Civil War general, still inhabited the family's old decaying plantation mansion, a "square, paintless house with its rotting portico." Its prewar cotton fields and pastures had been sold to settle family debts and were now part of a golf course.[53] When he became president in 1933, Franklin Roosevelt was shocked to learn that many sections of the South still lacked basic twentieth-century amenities such as electricity and running water. Few Southerners owned trucks or automobiles. The 1936 novel and classic 1939 film *Gone with the Wind*, which presented a romanticized view of the Old South's plantation culture, resonated with

Southern audiences who still sensed, more than seven decades later, the economic and environmental damage incurred by the South during the Civil War.

In 1967, during another war that divided the United States, not geographically but philosophically and spiritually, Lorraine Schneider, a Californian born in 1925, designed and marketed a popular poster whose image also found its way onto T-shirts and car bumper stickers. Schneider's print showed a flower and the words "War is not healthy for children and other living things." Her saying certainly applies to the most environmentally destructive war in U.S. history, the Civil War. Ironically, however, perhaps the environmental carnage that took place during the Civil War is partly responsible, as some twenty-first-century environmental historians suggest, for the advancement of a nature preservation movement in the United States.[54] Lincoln, who waged a total war to prevent his nation from dividing, did formulate some environmental conservation programs during his presidency that had long-term beneficial effects.

THE FRUITFUL SOURCE OF
ADVANTAGE TO ALL OUR PEOPLE

The Civil War dominated Abraham Lincoln's presidency. War tension was already in the air when he swore his presidential oath on March 4, 1861, and the conflict began a month after he took office. The war continued through the end of his presidency. During his term in office, Lincoln's main goals were to win the war, to reunite the fractured Union, and later, to abolish slavery forever in the United States. Lincoln had little time or political energy to devote to other issues and causes. Nonetheless, even a president whose term in office is dominated by a great war has other duties and concerns—some routine, like choosing cabinet officers and foreign ministers, and others more politically complicated, like managing economic and foreign policy and working with Congress on legislation. The conservation and preservation of the nation's natural environment was not at the top of Lincoln's presidential agenda when he took office; his administration and military leaders would wage a total war that did significant damage to the American natural environment during his four years in office. But the ecologically catastrophic Civil War is not the final chapter in Lincoln's environmental biography. Perhaps the terrible environmental carnage wrought by the war opened Lincoln and the nation to a restoration and renewal ethic that resulted in some measures to enhance the American natural environment during a time of war and laid the groundwork for conservation initiatives that came after Lincoln's death.

Even before the war and Lincoln's presidency, an environmental preservation and conservation movement, or at least a critique of the environmental effects wrought by industrialization, was under way in the United States. (*Environment* became an English word describing the natural landscape in the 1830s.[1]) This movement began with solitary voices who operated, for the most part, outside or on the fringes of the political system: William Cullen Bryant, writing poems that highlighted the beauty of nature and advocating for a great public park in New York City in the 1840s, and Henry David Thoreau, calling attention to the harmful effects of dams on migratory fish in New England rivers and later keeping a chronicle of his twenty-six-month stay in a one-room cabin in the woods on the shores of Walden Pond in Concord, Massachusetts, published as *Walden* in 1854.

Herman Melville is best known for *Moby-Dick,* his 1851 novel about a whaleship captain's unsuccessful attempt to conquer nature, symbolized by the great white whale that destroys the captain, Ahab, and his shipmates. Two years later, while Thoreau was writing his book about his joyful life in the natural environment at Walden Pond, Melville published "Bartleby, the Scrivener: A Story of Wall Street," the sad tale of a melancholy clerk laboring in a New York City law office. Bartleby is "walled-in" at his urban workplace. His desk sits near a wall, behind "a high green folding screen"; a window offers Bartleby only a view of a large brick building three feet away. His work—laboriously hand-copying legal texts during the days before typewriters or carbon paper—is uninspiring.[2] Bartleby becomes depressed in his sterile environment, and he suffers from what twenty-first-century psychologists might call nature-deficit disorder.[3] Living on Wall Street, Bartleby has no contact with the natural environment, which has been gradually disappearing as buildings have replaced trees and green spaces in the landscape of New York's financial district. At the story's conclusion, Bartleby gives up on work and life; he is arrested as a vagrant and dies within the walls of New York City's infamous Tombs Prison. Bartleby is a victim in a society that gives priority to financial profits, symbolized by the story's Wall Street setting, over the natural environment.

In 1831, a rural cemetery movement began with the opening of Mount Auburn Cemetery outside of Boston. Mount Auburn quickly became one of the top tourist attractions of the Boston area. Part of Mount Auburn's appeal was a "culture of death" that prevailed at the time, a fascination with the experience of death that went beyond its religious dimension and prompted people to visit cemeteries to engage in personal reflection. But Mount Auburn also offered Boston residents a grassy landscape and trees, an opportunity to escape the confines of the city and enjoy an environmentally pleasing place at a time when the city was becoming more heavily populated and more developed. After Mount Auburn opened, rural cemeteries were created outside of other cities, giving urban residents an opportunity to experience the natural world. When Sleepy Hollow Cemetery opened in Concord, Massachusetts, in 1855, Ralph Waldo Emerson, the transcendentalist philosopher and writer, appropriately offered the dedication address. The establishment of the cemetery at the Gettysburg battlefield, where Lincoln gave his most famous address, is part of this rural cemetery movement.[4] Lincoln is buried in such a cemetery, set, when it was created, on the outskirts of Springfield, Illinois.

American painters joined American writers and landscape architects in highlighting the beauty of the natural world and conveying the need to protect it in a rapidly industrializing society. The Hudson River School of painters, which included Thomas Cole, Frederic Edwin Church, George Inness, and Asher Brown Durand, used landscape painting both to pay homage to the nation's natural beauty and to critique its loss. A preferred venue for this group of painters was New York's Catskill Mountains, a place of stunning natural beauty. Cole, generally considered to be the founder of the Hudson River School, was an Englishman by birth; his family hailed from Lancashire, a region that experienced great environmental decline when the Industrial Revolution took hold in Great Britain in the eighteenth century. Cole, who had come to the United States as a child, feared that the same natural degeneration that had occurred in areas of Great Britain was taking place in his new country. Cole's sacred Catskills, for example, were undergoing serious deforestation because of the lumber and leather tanning industries. Tanning required an acidic chemical such as the tannin found in the bark of hemlock trees, which were plentiful in the Catskills in the early nineteenth century. Cole used his canvases to convey his concerns. An 1837 landscape painting, *View on the Catskill—Early Autumn*, for example, depicts Catskill Creek winding through a tree-lined landscape with two picnickers taking in the impressive natural beauty. *River in the Catskills*, painted six years later, depicts a similar scene. But there are fewer trees, and the foreground shows tree stumps and chopped tree trunks and limbs littering the landscape. In the background, a locomotive, spewing smoke, crosses a bridge erected across the river.[5] Machines have entered Cole's garden paradise. George Inness's *The Lackawanna Valley*, painted in 1856, conveys a similar theme. A locomotive, the powerful symbol of the Industrial Revolution, chugs through a natural landscape littered with tree stumps. The trees presumably were felled to create the locomotive's path and to fuel its engine.

Cole also used poetry to convey his environmental concerns. His poem "The Lament of the Forest," published in the *Knickerbocker* magazine in 1841, presents an idyllic mountain scene—"Forests of shadowy pine, hemlock and beech, / And oak and maple ever beautiful"—that gives way to human conquest:

> Then all was harmony and peace; but MAN
> Arose—he who now vaunts antiquity—
> He the destroyer—and in the sacred shades
> Of the far East began destruction's work.

In "A few short years!—these valleys, greenly clad, / . . . Shall naked glare beneath the scorching sun," and "No more the deer shall haunt these bosky glens, / Nor the pert squirrel chatter near his store."[6] The final lines of the poem offer the forest's lament mentioned in the title. Man, in Cole's view, has become nature's destroyer; hence, forests must be protected from his destructive impulses.

During this time, the pre–Civil War decades, Lincoln's Whig Party was still avidly advocating its program of internal improvements and supporting American manufacturing with no regard for the environmental effects. Eventually, however, some politicians began to hear the voices of the writers, landscape architects, and artists. For example, lawmakers in New York State eventually listened to William Cullen Bryant and others who were clamoring for a grand central park in New York City. Between 1820 and 1850, the population of the city had more than quadrupled, from just under 125,000 to more than 500,000 residents. New York had supplanted Philadelphia as the city with the largest population in the United States. Immigration was certainly a factor in this population rise. The great potato famine that gripped Ireland in the late 1840s prompted thousands of Irish to emigrate to the United States; many settled in East Coast port cities like New York and Boston. Buildings arose to house the rising population. Trees fell and green spaces disappeared. Along with Bryant, many New Yorkers were urging the creation of a grand city park like the ones in London, Paris, and other European cities, a place preserved from development, where city dwellers could go for walks, carriage rides, and picnics in a natural setting. In 1857, the New York legislature selected a seven-hundred-acre plot of land in the center of Manhattan, from 59th through 106th Streets, for what would be named Central Park. A design competition was held, and Frederick Law Olmsted and Calvert Vaux, two landscape architects, won the competition to design the new park, which opened in 1858. Central Park, with its green lawns, trees, and pond, provided New York City residents and visitors a natural place of escape from the crowded urban streets.

Perhaps the first national environmental protest in the United States took place in the 1850s. The impetus for the protest was the downing of two California giant sequoia trees, also known as Sierra redwoods. On June 27, 1853, California gold miners chopped down a three-hundred-foot-tall, 1,244-year-old giant redwood in Calaveras County, California. The tree choppers, who labored for three weeks to fell the tree, intended to extract a large section of the tree's bark and exhibit it, attracting paying customers who had never seen such an enormous tree. A year later, another giant sequoia was axed, and its bark was displayed in the United States and later shipped to England for exhibit there. The two trees received names: the first, Mammoth Tree, and the second, Mother of the Forest. As word of the felling of the first tree spread, the press reacted harshly. An article in the local *Sonora Herald* asserted that killing the tree "is much to be deprecated." The *Placer Times and Transcript*, published in San Francisco, expressed shock at "the vandalism and barbarity of flaying that giant of the woods." Word of the first tree's felling spread. In October, Maturin Ballou, the editor of *Gleason's Pictorial Drawing Room Companion*, published in Boston, was traveling in California and heard of the fate of Mammoth Tree. He condemned the action in the pages of his magazine: "To our mind it seems a cruel idea, a perfect desecration, to cut down such a splendid tree" to be shipped off "for a shilling show!" Ballou added: "We hope that no one will conceive the idea of purchasing the Niagara Falls with the same purpose!" When word of the felling of the Mother of the Forest spread, the *New York Herald*, in an article in December 1855, urged lawmakers to end the slaughter of California's redwoods: "We say that Congress should interpose, upon the presumption that these trees are public property [and] are on the public lands of California. . . . We repeat, that it is the duty of the State of California, of Congress, and of all good citizens, to protect and to preserve these California monuments of the capabilities of our American soil."[7] At this time, the nation was hotly debating the slavery issue, and Lincoln's new Republican Party had just formed to deal with the issue, but still, California's tree protest had stretched across the nation and reached the East Coast.

The idea of Congress preserving land for public recreational use was a new concept in the mid-nineteenth century. During his presidency thirty years earlier, John Quincy Adams had set aside fifteen hundred acres of oak trees on Santa Rosa Island in Florida's Pensacola Bay for use as masts for the navy's ships, not for conservation.[8] An early voice for the preservation of wilderness areas as public parks was George Catlin, a Pennsylvania artist and travel writer who journeyed in 1832 along the Missouri River, in present-day South Dakota, and recorded his experiences. Much of Catlin's artwork focused on Native American life. On his trip, Catlin witnessed Native Americans slaying buffalo and imagined, instead, the animals "preserved in their pristine beauty and wildness, in a *magnificent park*, where the world could see for all ages to come, the native Indian in his classic attire, galloping his wild horse, with sinewy bow, and shield and lance, amid the fleeting herds of elks and buffaloes. . . . A *nation's Park*, containing man and beast, in all the wild freshness of their natural beauty!"[9]

As the great California redwood protest crossed the nation, Thoreau added his voice to the call for the preservation of natural landscapes. He had traveled to Maine in 1848, 1853, and 1857. In the summer of 1858, the *Atlantic Monthly* published an account that Thoreau had written of his 1853 trip under the title "Chesuncook," the name of a Maine lake that he had visited. In the article, Thoreau lamented that "so few ever come to the woods to see how the pine lives and grows and spires, lifting its evergreen arms to the light,—to see its true success; but most are content to behold it in the shape of many broad boards brought to the market, and deem *that* its true success!" He asked, rhetorically, if it were the lumberman and leather tanner who are the friends of the tree. "No! no!" he responded, "it is the poet; he it is who makes the truest use of the pine,—who does not fondle it with an axe, nor tickle it with a saw, nor stroke it with a plane." Thoreau called for "national preserves," to be used "not for idle sport or food, but for inspiration and our own true re-creation."[10] When Thoreau's article appeared in the *Atlantic Monthly*, Lincoln was preparing for his debates with Stephen Douglas in his attempt to wrest from Douglas his Illinois U.S. Senate seat in the forthcoming November election. Lincoln's mind was focused on politics and the slavery issue, not the preservation of places of natural beauty.

The year after the *Atlantic Monthly* published Thoreau's "Chesuncook," Horace Greeley, the influential Whig editor of the *New York Tribune*, journeyed from New York to San Francisco. While in California, Greeley visited Yosemite Valley, about 125 miles southeast of where Mammoth Tree was cut down. Greeley published an account of his trip in his newspaper, and a year later, he published the account in book form, titled *An Overland Journey from New York to San Francisco in the Summer of 1859*. Greeley highlighted Yosemite's stunning natural beauty, and he became a strong public advocate for the preservation of America's forests.[11] On the eve of the Civil War, nature conservation was gaining attention as a national issue.

Despite the national emergency brought on by the war, environ-mental conservation gained some traction as a political issue during Lincoln's tenure in office. In March 1864, as the war raged east of the Mississippi River, Frederick Law Olmsted made a trip to Yosemite Valley. Olmsted sent a detailed report of his trip along with photo-graphs to California's U.S. senator John Conness. Conness, who had been serving in the California state assembly when the Mammoth Tree and Mother of the Forest fell a decade earlier, was receptive to Olmsted's report. He circulated the photographs of Yosemite Valley to his colleagues in Congress and began crafting a bill that would prevent the development or commercial use of Yosemite Valley and nearby Mariposa Big Tree Grove and preserve the area as a public park. In May 1864, Conness introduced his bill to Congress.[12]

If Senator Conness's bill received approval in Congress, it would have to be signed into law by President Lincoln. Back in his days as a member of the Whig Party, Lincoln had supported the sale of government-owned land to private citizens for development. The sale of federal land to settlers was a way of populating new territories, settling the American continent, and securing funds for the Whigs' program of internal improvements. In the 1830s and 1840s, various homestead acts offered citizens the opportunity to purchase acre-age from the federal government, or from states, at low prices if the citizens pledged to live on and farm the land for a specified period of time. Millions of acres of federal lands were sold to settlers and to railroad companies during this time period.[13] Just before Lincoln took office as president, he offered his support for the federal Home-stead Act, which had been working its way through Congress in the final months of James Buchanan's presidency. When Lincoln's train from Springfield, Illinois, to Washington stopped in Cincinnati on February 12, 1861, Lincoln told a crowd gathered at the train station to greet him, "In regard to the Homestead Law, I have to say that in so far as the Government lands can be disposed of, I am in favor of cutting up wild lands into parcels, so that every poor man may have a home." Lincoln signed the Homestead Act into law in May 1862. In his annual address to Congress, delivered in December 1863, Lincoln reported that the federal government had, in the past year and three months, sold 3,841,549 acres of public land, 1,456,514 acres of which had been disposed of through the Homestead Act.[14] The Homestead Act disposed of federal land by putting it into private hands. Much of the land went to farmers, but some went to land speculators and to railroad companies as well for industrial development. Senator Conness's Yosemite legislation, however, was unique, proposing to conserve and preserve federal land from any kind of development, agricultural or industrial. The land in Yosemite Valley would be set aside for public use and recreation; it would not become available for private ownership.[15]

But early in his presidency, Lincoln might have signaled, in a routine memo to Congress, that he was open to strategies for conserving and preserving natural environments. In July 1861, four months after Lincoln had taken office, his secretary of state, William Seward, received a request from the British minister assigned to Washington regarding the management of fisheries along the northeast coast. Lincoln's memo to Congress indicated that management of the fisheries met his approval: "As the United States have, in common with Great Britain and France, a deep interest in the preservation and development of the fisheries adjacent to the Northeastern coast and Islands of this continent, it seems proper that we should concert with the Governments of those countries such measures as may be conducive to those important objects." Lincoln forwarded to Congress a copy of the correspondence between the British minister and Seward and recommended "the appointment of a Joint Commission to inquire into the matter, in order that such ulterior measures may be adopted as may be advisable for the objects proposed. Such legislation is recommended as may be necessary to enable the Executive to provide for a Commissioner on behalf of the United States." Congress sent Lincoln's proposal to the Senate's Foreign Relations Committee, and action was postponed indefinitely.[16] Nonetheless, Lincoln indicated in this routine memo that he was open to the conservation and preservation of natural resources, in this case fisheries.

During his presidency, Lincoln also became more interested in West Coast issues. When he began his political career in Illinois as a Whig in the 1830s, Lincoln had little interest in political issues of concern to citizens who lived in the West.[17] But the Mexican War of 1846–48, the California gold rush of 1849, the push for California statehood in 1850, and issues concerning the Oregon Territory had made him more aware of the political climate of the West Coast. Lincoln was also the friend of Noah Brooks, a California newspaper correspondent. The two men had met when they both lived in Illinois, and Brooks resided in Washington during Lincoln's presidency, covering the nation's capital for Sacramento's *Daily Union*. Brooks would certainly have kept Lincoln abreast of West Coast political issues such as Senator Conness's effort to preserve Yosemite Valley.[18]

Conness's proposed law, the Yosemite Valley Grant Act, would preserve federal land rather than distribute it for private ownership and use as various homestead legislations did. Technically, the act would deed federal land in Yosemite Valley and Mariposa Big Tree Grove to the state of California for preservation from development. The bill stated that "the said State shall accept this grant upon the express conditions that the premises shall be held for public use, resort, and recreation" and "shall be inalienable for all time."[19] The bill passed both houses of Congress and was signed into law by Lincoln on June 30, 1864. Lincoln, who knew both Horace Greeley and Frederick Law Olmsted, had likely read their reports on Yosemite and understood the need for preserving it from development. The Yosemite Valley Grant Act was unprecedented in U.S. history. It also foreshadowed the birth of the U.S. National Park System.[20]

In the summer of 1865, after Lincoln's death, Olmsted was appointed to compose a report to the governor of California on the land set aside by the Yosemite Valley Grant Act. His report stressed the beauty of the natural landscape. "No photograph or series of photographs, no paintings, ever prepare a visitor so that he is not taken by surprise," Olmsted wrote. He went on to speculate about the benefits of visiting places of natural beauty: "It is a scientific fact that the occasional contemplation of natural scenes of an impressive character, particularly if this contemplation occurs in connection with relief from ordinary cares, change of air and change of habits, is favorable to the health and vigor of men and especially to the health and vigor of their intellect." The lack of recreation that involves contact with

The Yosemite Valley Grant Act of 1864, signed into law by President Lincoln, protected California's Yosemite Valley, a place of stunning natural beauty. Library of Congress.

the natural world, on the other hand, in Olmsted's view, can cause "softening of the brain, paralysis, palsy, monomania, or insanity," as well as "nervous excitability, moroseness, melancholy or irascibility, incapacitating the subject for the proper exercise of the intellectual and moral forces."[21]

The Yosemite Valley Grant Act would have far-reaching environmental effects. So would another initiative concerning the natural

environment that Lincoln took as president during the Civil War—
the reorganization of the U.S. Department of Agriculture. Since
1839, an Agricultural Division had existed within the U.S. Patent
Office, which, when Lincoln became president, was housed in the
Department of Interior. Lincoln saw the need for the Agricultural
Division to become more independent and for its work to receive
more attention. In his first annual message to the Congress, delivered
in December 1861, Lincoln signaled his intention to reorganize the
Agricultural Division:

> Agriculture, confessedly the largest interest of the nation, has,
> not a department, nor a bureau, but a clerkship only, assigned
> to it in the government. While it is fortunate that this great
> interest is so independent in its nature as to not have demanded
> and extorted more from the government, I respectfully ask
> Congress to consider whether something more cannot be given
> voluntarily with general advantage.
>
> Annual reports exhibiting the condition of our agriculture,
> commerce, and manufactures would present a fund of informa-
> tion of great practical value to the country. While I make no
> suggestion as to details, I venture the opinion that an agricul-
> tural and statistical bureau might profitably be organized.[22]

On May 15, 1862, Lincoln signed a bill to establish the Department of Agriculture. In his annual report to Congress delivered in
December of that year, Lincoln highlighted the department's creation as an "immediate benefit of a large class of our most valuable
citizens" and "the fruitful source of advantage to all our people."[23]
Pre–Civil War farming methods had resulted in serious deforestation
and soil erosion. A better-organized and better-funded Department
of Agriculture could enhance the environment by developing and
encouraging the use of more ecologically sound methods of farming.

In his 1865 report for the Department of Agriculture titled "American Forests: Their Destruction and Preservation," Frederick Starr
Jr. highlighted the widespread damage done to American woodlands during the Civil War. Starr's report was exactly the kind of
scientific study that Lincoln had anticipated when he enhanced the

Department of Agriculture in 1862. Starr suggested that the nation should care for damaged forests as it cared for the war's wounded soldiers and that part of reuniting the nation after the war would be to restore the natural environment. "Let us then inquire, why government should aid such efforts?" he asked. "*The work is national.* Every part of the land suffers together."[24] Healing the damaged natural landscape might help heal the nation's war wounds. In November 1863 at Gettysburg, Lincoln spoke of a "new birth of freedom" for the nation.[25] He was referring to the abolition of American slavery, triggered by the Emancipation Proclamation issued eleven months earlier. But after the war, as Starr suggested, the country would also need an environmental rebirth to repair the extensive damage done to the natural landscape during the war.

Another piece of legislation signed by Lincoln during his presidency, the Morrill Act, would have a positive effect on the nation's agriculture. Named for Vermont congressman Justin Morrill, the act allocated to each state, excluding the states that had voted to secede from the Union, thirty thousand acres of federal land for each state's member of Congress to create colleges devoted to the study of agriculture and the mechanical arts. The land could be granted to both existing and new schools. Lincoln's presidential predecessor, James Buchanan, had vetoed a similar bill in 1859. Both houses of Congress passed the Morrill Act in June 1862. On July 2, Lincoln signed the bill. These colleges would test and develop new environmentally sustainable methods of farming and engineering and teach these methods to their students. Faculty members teaching at these schools would author books and articles on their agricultural and engineering research. A list of the early land grant colleges includes Cornell University, Iowa State University, Kansas State University, Rutgers University, Pennsylvania State University, Michigan State University, the University of Maine, the University of Kentucky, and the University of Maryland, all of which were designated before the Civil War ended. The land grant schools also played a role in reshaping higher education in the United States. The Ivy League tradition of education, developed at America's first colleges and universities, stressed classical learning—philosophy, classical languages such as

Latin and ancient Greek, classical literature, and mathematics. These land grant colleges and universities would offer curricula to train students to develop practical skills and knowledge, eventually making a college or university a place where students could study business, nursing, and other practical disciplines. After the Civil War, the Southern states that had joined the Confederacy also became beneficiaries of the Morrill Act.

One twenty-first-century environmental historian claims that the passage of the Morrill Act and the creation of the Department of Agriculture were "monumental developments in the environmental history of the nation's farmlands and deserve to sit at the center of our assessment of the Civil War's larger environmental legacies."[26] Lincoln, the farm boy who walked away from farming when he reached adulthood, never planning to return, signed, as president, landmark legislation that advanced the scientific study of American agriculture. Perhaps Lincoln's childhood and young adulthood immersion in farming had dovetailed with an interest in science that he developed through his adult reading. He regularly read *Annual of Scientific Discovery*, which began publication in 1850.[27] Edited by David Wells, this annual publication collected articles on the most recent scientific discoveries and developments in chemistry, zoology, geology, astronomy, and the other natural sciences. One of Lincoln's New Salem friends, Mentor Graham, reported to Lincoln's Springfield law partner and early biographer, William Herndon, that as a young man, Lincoln "devoted more time to reading the scripture, books on science and comments on law and to the acquisition of Knowledge of men and things than any man I ever knew." Another New Salem acquaintance, Robert Rutledge, made a similar observation: "He studied first Kirkhams Grammar and the Arithmetic, then Natural philosophy, Astronomy & Chemistry, then Surveying, and Law."[28] Herndon recalled Lincoln's excitement over Robert Chambers's *Vestiges of the Natural History of Creation*, a study published fifteen years before Charles Darwin's landmark 1859 *Origin of Species*, which suggested that animal species have evolved into their present forms: "A gentleman in Springfield gave him [Lincoln] a book called, I believe, 'Vestiges of Creation,' which interested him so much that he read it through. The volume was published in Edinburgh, and undertook to demonstrate the doctrine of development or evolution. The treatise interested him greatly, and he was deeply impressed with the notion of the so-called 'universal law'—evolution."[29]

In March 1863, Lincoln signed a bill, passed by Congress, to incorporate the National Academy of Sciences. The new law created the academy, comprising a group of fifty distinguished American scientists, which could be called on by any branch of the federal government to investigate any scientific subject and report its findings. On the 150th anniversary of the National Academy of Sciences in 2013, Neil deGrasse Tyson, an astrophysicist at New York's Hayden Planetarium, delivered a speech acknowledging Lincoln's role in the academy's creation. "While most remember honest Abe for war and peace, and slavery and freedom, the time has come to remember him for setting our Nation on a course of scientifically enlightened governance, without which we may perish from this Earth," stated Tyson.[30]

The most influential environmental impact statement delivered during Lincoln's presidency came not from him but from one of his foreign ministers. In 1864, Lincoln's minister to Italy, George Perkins Marsh, published *Man and Nature, or Physical Geography as Modified by Human Affairs*, considered by many twenty- and twenty-first-century environmental scientists as America's first comprehensive study of ecology. Marsh was born in Vermont in 1801 and educated at Dartmouth. After college, he studied the law and became an attorney. Politically, Marsh was, like Lincoln, a Whig, and he served three terms in the U.S. House of Representatives, his final two years with Lincoln. But Marsh's great love was for foreign languages—he spoke and wrote in many—so he switched his career focus from legislation to foreign diplomacy. He was appointed as minister to the Ottoman Empire by President Zachary Taylor in 1849, returned home after five years in that service, then was appointed as minister to Italy by Lincoln when he took office in 1861. Marsh served in that role until his death in 1882.

Marsh had a lifelong interest in the natural environment. Growing up in Vermont, he had witnessed how the lumbering business had desecrated the state's forests. In 1857, he completed a study for the governor and the state legislature of Vermont on the state's fish population. In that report, he warned that the extensive damming of Vermont's rivers hampered proper soil drainage and that deforestation was leading to climate change.[31] When Marsh was sent to Italy by Lincoln, he began work on *Man and Nature*. The book included chapters on animals, woods, waters, and sands. His objective in writing the book was "to indicate the character and approximately, the extent of the changes produced by human action in the physical conditions of the globe we inhabit." He explained, for example, how the felling of trees could affect a region's soil and climate. "But man is everywhere a disturbing agent," he wrote. "Wherever he plants his foot, the harmonies of nature are turned to discords. The proportions and accommodations which insured the stability of existing arrangements are overthrown." Marsh warned that the earth, "stripped of its vegetable glebe, grows less and less productive. . . . Gradually it becomes altogether barren." He sharply criticized the methods of farming employed by many American farmers—clearing woodlands to create farm fields, planting crops for several seasons until the soil was nutritionally exhausted, then moving on to seek fresher soil. Marsh claimed that land used by human beings and then abandoned did not return, over time, to its natural state; it became barren and impoverished, a wasteland.[32] Undoubtedly, Lincoln's effort to foster the scientific study of agriculture through the Morrill Act and his enhancement of the Department of Agriculture would have had Marsh's stamp of approval.

Even though *Man and Nature* was laced with scientific jargon and information that might not be easily comprehended by readers without an education or background in science, the book was an almost instant publishing success. During its first few months in publication, at the height of the Civil War, one hundred thousand copies of the book were sold.[33] The book's main theme—how humans have damaged the natural environment—might have struck a chord with American readers at a time when war was fracturing their nation and laying waste to its natural landscape. But *Man and Nature* was not simply a stern jeremiad, warning humankind of the demise of the earth's physical landscape. It offered a message of hope: if the natural environment were managed properly, rather than improperly or haphazardly or not at all, then environmental destruction could be stopped and the environment preserved and healed. This is a theme that Catlin, Thoreau, Olmsted, Cole, and others had sounded in the years leading up to the Civil War. Politicians including Conness and Lincoln had heard their message and acted on it, signaling that government could play a significant role in conserving the country's natural environment.

An incident in his final days signals that Lincoln might have been thinking about the damaging effects that four years of civil war had on the American natural landscape. In her autobiography, Elizabeth Keckley, a former slave who was Mary Lincoln's seamstress and companion, recorded an incident that took place in Petersburg, Virginia, in April 1865, near the end of the Civil War. Lincoln and his wife visited Petersburg after it came under Union control. The city and its surrounding natural landscape had suffered damage during the Union siege of Petersburg, which lasted more than nine months. Departing from Petersburg, Lincoln insisted that his visiting party stop to view an oak tree on the outskirts of the city that had attracted his attention earlier. According to Keckley, Lincoln and the members of his party took a second look "at the isolated and magnificent specimen of the stately grandeur of the forest. Every member of the party was only too willing to accede to the President's request, and the visit to the oak tree was made, and much enjoyed."[34] Perhaps Lincoln admired the oak tree for its resilience during the long siege of Petersburg. Perhaps the tree suggested nature's endurance despite the damage wrought upon natural landscapes by human beings. Perhaps Lincoln sensed that the natural environment, symbolized by the tree, would need care in the aftermath of the devastating war.

Before Lincoln's presidency, voices extolling the virtues of the American natural landscape and critiquing agricultural practices and industrial forces that threatened it operated, for the most part, outside the political arena. They wrote books, poems, and essays; created paintings; and privately sought places of natural beauty to satisfy their craving for a relationship with nature. By the time Lincoln took office as president, however, politicians were beginning to hear these voices and understand the environmental issues that they raised. New York lawmakers created Central Park. Senator John Conness of California sensed a threat to his state's giant redwood trees and crafted federal legislation to protect at least some of them. Lincoln, during the Civil War, which dominated his presidency and caused great damage to the American natural environment, supported initiatives to protect natural landscapes, encourage more environmentally sustainable agricultural practices, and empower scientists to use their discipline to solve national problems. At the time of his tragic death, Lincoln's environmental sensitivities were apparently still evolving.

EPILOGUE

When Abraham Lincoln was assassinated six weeks into his second presidential term, the Civil War was ending, and he and his administration were facing major postwar issues. He needed to reunite the nation politically—to bring the South back into the governing process by persuading the defeated Confederate states to send representatives to Congress and become part of a politically reunited Union. Lincoln needed to develop a plan to deal with four million newly freed slaves, most of whom had to be housed, fed, and employed. His administration had just begun to address that problem by establishing the Freedmen's Bureau at the start of his second term. He also needed to initiate a plan to rebuild the South, many areas of which had suffered extensive physical and economic damage, especially during the last two years of the war, when Lincoln's top generals, with their commander in chief's approval, waged a total war on the Confederacy. A Lincoln postwar second presidential term might have yielded important initiatives and developments in a variety of other areas—civil rights, land policy, agricultural policy, foreign policy, policies concerning Native Americans. Dealing with the defeated South, Lincoln would also have had to confront environmental issues—how to begin to heal the South's war-damaged natural landscape.

No one can say exactly what post–Civil War environmental policies and programs Lincoln might have initiated had he lived through his second presidential term. Although the word *environment* had slipped into the English language in the 1830s, *environmental policy* did not become a term until the 1960s, a century after Lincoln's death.[1] Presidents elected before the Civil War did not have clearly articulated environmental plans or policies. But having charted the environmental path on which Lincoln journeyed during his lifetime, we can follow that path and see where it led his nation in the decades following the Civil War.

In his young adulthood, Lincoln was part of a major shift in American environmental history: the movement of Americans off the farms and into towns and cities. When Lincoln was born in 1809, 90 percent of Americans lived on farms. One hundred years later, a little more than one-third of Americans lived on farms, and that percentage declined further during the twentieth century.[2] During the nineteenth century, millions of Americans, like Lincoln, divorced themselves from direct and daily contact with the natural environment. They no longer worked the land, grew their own food, or tended livestock; they purchased food in shops and markets, supplied by local farmers and later by large agricultural companies that eventually learned how to package, can, and later freeze produce for purchase by nonfarming consumers. Millions of immigrants who came to the United States during Lincoln's lifetime and the decades following his death never owned land to farm. Today many Americans still identify as farmers, and millions of Americans tend backyard, rooftop, and community vegetable gardens, but many people living in the United States in the twenty-first century have never created a garden plot, planted a vegetable, weeded a garden, or picked their own produce. Lincoln was part of a national trend away from farming that began during his lifetime and continued long after his death. Lincoln did sign into law the Homestead Act of 1862 to make farmlands available to small farmers, but much of the available land covered by the act fell into the hands of land speculators and railroad companies. Despite the passage of the Homestead Act, the trend away from farming continued in the decades after Lincoln died.

But as president, Lincoln helped advance two grand agricultural initiatives—the enhancement of the Department of Agriculture and the establishment and funding of the land grant colleges and universities—and both bore fruit. In 1876, the Office of Special Agent was created within the Department of Agriculture to monitor American forestland and form policies for its prudent use and preservation. This office was expanded into the Division of Forestry in 1881. The Department of Agriculture achieved cabinet status in 1889.

Deforestation had been a serious environmental problem during Lincoln's entire lifetime, and it continued during the post–Civil War rebuilding effort. Even before the war, Henry David Thoreau, Thomas Cole, George Perkins Marsh, and others had raised serious concerns over the reduction of American woodlands. Over time, however, the work of the Forestry Division, which evolved into the U.S. Forest Service and was strengthened by the Wilderness Act of 1964, has been impressive. In 2013, the *Boston Globe* reported that 80 percent of New England is now covered with trees. In the mid-1800s, only 30 to 40 percent of New England was forested. Populations of deer, moose, beavers, wildcats, hawks, woodpeckers, and other wildlife dependent on forest habitats have rebounded in New England with astonishing speed.[3] A variety of factors combined to curb deforestation, including the national movement away from farming and the shift from wood to coal, oil, natural gas, and other materials for heating and fuel, but the work of the U.S. Forest Service has surely played a major role in protecting American woodlands. The Morrill Act, Lincoln's other prominent agricultural initiative, was updated in 1890 to include the former Confederate states. Seventy American colleges and universities ultimately received land grants under the Morrill Act to expand their study of agriculture and engineering. Students at the land grant colleges and universities have studied fertilization, soil sustainability, plant and soil diseases, and other topics related to agriculture.

But the scientific study of American agriculture, initiated by legislation passed during Lincoln's administration, did not guarantee that the nation's agricultural practices would consistently remain environmentally sound. During and after World War I, American wheat was aggressively grown and harvested in Texas, Oklahoma, Kansas, and other states to meet a high world demand. As a result, millions of acres of soils in some wheat states became nutritionally depleted, turning some wheat-growing regions into agricultural wastelands. Several years of drought and severe windstorms followed in some of these regions, creating the 1930s Dust Bowl, poignantly captured in Dorothea Lange's photographs; Woody Guthrie's ballads; and John Steinbeck's 1939 novel, *The Grapes of Wrath*, and the film based on the novel released the following year.

After World War II, the Department of Agriculture was responsible for spreading the chemical DDT on American farmlands and forests to eliminate insect pests. In 1962, Rachel Carson, an aquatic biologist and nature writer, published an environmental critique on the use of DDT and other pesticides, first in a series of articles in the *New Yorker* magazine and then in her influential book, *Silent Spring*. Carson's book describes how the Department of Agriculture made a significant effort in the 1950s to wipe out gypsy moths in New England and fire ants in Alabama by covering large sections of farmlands and woodlands with DDT, which contaminated the natural landscape. Birds and other wildlife were poisoned, and in bird species higher up the food chain, consumption of greater quantities of DDT resulted in eggshells that were too thin to support the embryos. When spread over farmlands, DDT got into the food chain, potentially causing cancers and other serious diseases.[4] *Silent Spring* kicked off an environmental movement that spanned the final decades of the twentieth century and continued into the twenty-first.

After he left the family farm and entered law and politics, Lincoln became firmly committed to support for internal improvements. Lincoln's first articulated political position was the need for government financing of roads, bridges, railroads, and canals, which were a means of mastering the natural environment, unifying the geographically expanding nation, and allowing products to be efficiently shipped across the country. The nation's commitment to internal improvement programs continued long after Lincoln's death. In 1869, the transcontinental railroad, which Lincoln had enthusiastically supported during his presidential term, was completed, and train networks crisscrossed the country. Over the next several decades, railroads became a major form of transportation for American travelers and for American products shipped across the nation. After

World War II, airplane travel became popular, and Americans began purchasing automobiles in great numbers, forcing the closure of many railroad networks. In the 1950s, President Dwight Eisenhower promoted the creation of the U.S. Interstate Highway System, an internal improvement project that prompted many Americans to travel by car instead of train. But many abandoned train routes have gained new life in the twenty-first century as walking, jogging, and bicycle paths. Often these rails-to-trails pathways wind through pleasing landscapes, connecting Americans to the natural environment.

The United States began one of its most impressive transportation projects in 1904, after it leased a swath of land from the newly formed nation of Panama, which had recently achieved independence from Colombia with American assistance. In the nineteenth century, France had attempted to build a canal there but failed. The American-built Panama Canal opened in 1914, enabling U.S. ships to travel from one coast to the other without having to circumvent the tip of South America. Had Lincoln, who wanted to be known as "the DeWitt Clinton of Illinois," lived into the twentieth century, he certainly would have strongly supported the effort to build the Panama Canal.

Some important and beloved American landmarks were internal improvement projects: the Brooklyn Bridge, on which construction began four years after the Civil War ended and which opened in 1883; the George Washington Bridge, which opened in 1931; the Hoover Dam, which opened in 1935; the Golden Gate Bridge, which opened in 1937; and the Grand Coulee Dam, which opened in 1942. Much grander in scale than the infrastructure projects that Lincoln and his contemporaries had imagined, these projects, like the ones in Lincoln's time, helped the American citizenry master the natural environment. They enabled citizens and vehicles to cross bodies of water, and they dammed and redirected rivers to create hydroelectric power. The Lincoln Tunnel, connecting New Jersey to New York City, opened in 1937, enabled vehicles to cross a river by going under it.

During the Great Depression, President Franklin Roosevelt used a program of internal improvements to get Americans working—the

Works Progress Administration, which built roads, bridges, schools, libraries, playgrounds, and other public facilities. Several million Americans worked on these projects. Internal improvements, now called infrastructure improvements, continue to be a winning political campaign issue in the United States. Many politicians across the political spectrum campaign for the improvement of roads and highways, bridges, tunnels, airports, and train stations to facilitate transportation and create jobs. Most infrastructure projects have an environmental impact, as they did in Lincoln's time. Minimally, green space is lost where airports and roadways are constructed. But today's infrastructure projects, unlike those in Lincoln's time, include environmental impact statements assessing how the project will affect its surrounding natural environment.

Contemporary infrastructure projects do sometimes raise environmental concerns and protests, as they did in Lincoln's time. In 2016, an oil pipeline under construction from North Dakota to Illinois met with stiff opposition from members of the tribe living on the Standing Rock Sioux Reservation in North Dakota, through which the pipeline would pass. Tribe members and their environmentalist supporters feared that the oil pipeline, designed to run under the Missouri River, the reservation's main source of drinking water, could leak and poison the water. As a result of the protests, construction on the pipeline was temporarily halted, and a new route was proposed. Work on the pipeline was eventually resumed.

Lincoln and his Whig and Republican parties strongly supported American manufacturing. American political leaders since Alexander Hamilton have argued that to maintain its independence, the United States would have to manufacture its own products for American consumers rather than rely on products imported from abroad. Lincoln's Whigs, and later the Republicans, supported high tariffs on imports to stimulate American manufacturing and encourage Americans to purchase domestically made products. The Industrial Revolution spanned Lincoln's lifetime and continued after it. In the decades after Lincoln's death, the United States became the world's industrial leader; its factories daily turned out products for domestic use and export—vehicles, household products and appliances, clothing, construction tools and materials, furniture. The industrialization of America, however, had serious environmental consequences—felt as early as the late eighteenth century, when Samuel Slater's mill on the Blackstone River in Rhode Island blocked salmon from swimming upstream into fresh water to spawn. By the twentieth century, many rivers including the Blackstone were polluted from poisonous factory waste and raw sewage dumped into rivers without treatment. America's factories caused air and other types of pollution as well. The Industrial Revolution that Lincoln had so strongly supported succeeded, but with a significant environmental cost.

No major wars have been fought on U.S. soil since the Civil War. For another twenty-five years after the Civil War, U.S. troops waged war against Native American tribes living in the Great Plains, but those wars were fairly limited in scope and caused less environmental damage than the Civil War. The United States fought two major wars in the twentieth century, but most of the carnage and environmental damage took place on European and Japanese soil. Hence, since the Civil War, the United States has been spared the horrendous environmental damage wrought by modern warfare. The only U.S. soil attacked during the two World Wars was the military base at Hawaii's Pearl Harbor. No American civil wars occurred after the one during Lincoln's term in office. His hope for "a lasting peace, among ourselves," expressed in his Second Inaugural Address, was sustained.[5] Nonetheless, in the spring and summer of 2017, Americans born more than a century after the Civil War ended clashed over the effort to remove monuments built in the South to honor Confederate war heroes such as Generals Robert E. Lee and Thomas "Stonewall" Jackson in New Orleans, Charlottesville, Virginia, and other Southern towns and cities.

The South's environment slowly healed after the Civil War. Its cotton-based economy and its natural landscape were severely damaged by the war. Plantations and farms had been destroyed by Union troops, and after the North won the war, the South's slaves were free, depriving cotton growers of their major supply of labor. Many former slaves remained in the South, working for hire or as sharecroppers, but in the early twentieth century, a Great Migration of former slaves and their descendants commenced, as millions of African Americans living in the South, denied their civil rights and unable to find work that provided a living wage, moved to the North. They settled in Detroit, Pittsburgh, Chicago, and other cities where industrial jobs were available for uneducated and minimally skilled workers. The South's landscape and agricultural economy eventually rebounded after the Civil War. At the end of the nineteenth century, the South's cotton production was triple what it had been in the 1860s.[6] In his Second Inaugural Address, Lincoln committed himself to binding up the nation's war wounds. Perhaps if Lincoln had lived to complete a second presidential term, those wounds would have healed more quickly.

A more energetic environmental movement commenced after the Civil War. In the 1870s, magazines for outdoor enthusiasts such as the *American Sportsman* and *Forest and Stream* began publication. Articles about fishing, hunting, hiking, and camping filled their pages, but these magazines also advocated the preservation of the natural landscapes where these outdoor activities took place. In 1887, Theodore Roosevelt and George Grinnell, the editor of *Forest and Stream*, organized the New York Boone and Crockett Club, which began advocating for the creation of a system of preserved national forests. Five years later, John Muir, a nature writer and strong advocate of environmental preservation, formed the influential Sierra Club, whose main mission was the protection of the natural environment.[7]

Lincoln's most far-reaching environmental initiative was the Yosemite Valley Grant Act. Setting aside federal land for "public use, resort, and recreation" was unprecedented before Lincoln signed the Yosemite legislation, and the protection of Yosemite Valley and Mariposa Big Tree Grove in California inspired conservationists across the United States. In 1871, Muir and other conservationists who had visited the land surrounding the Yellowstone River, which flows through Montana and Wyoming, began calling for the area's preservation. The following year, President Ulysses S. Grant signed into law a bill establishing Yellowstone National Park, the country's first national park. In 1890, Yosemite National Park was established, and the land deeded to California under the Yosemite Valley Grant Act was eventually added to it. More than fifty places of natural beauty have been designated as national parks, preserving them from settlement or development. In 1891, President Benjamin Harrison, responding to lobbying from conservationists, signed the Land Revision Act, giving the president authority to preserve U.S. forestland.[8] Today more than 150 forests have protection under this law.

Protecting natural landscapes such as Yosemite Valley was of great importance in U.S. environmental history, but equally important was the concept introduced by Lincoln when he signed the Yosemite legislation: the federal government would assume a role in *protecting* and *managing* the natural environment. Before the Civil War, the environmental ramifications of legislation were rarely considered. Through various homestead acts and other legislation, millions of acres of public lands were disposed of cheaply for use and development by farmers but also by railroad companies. Industrialists were free to treat the environment as they pleased without government interference. Railroad companies did not have to plant trees to compensate for the trees chopped down during railroad construction. Mills and factories did not have to consider the impact that their waste disposal might have on a river and its fish population.

American presidents who followed Lincoln—Grant, Harrison, Theodore and Franklin Roosevelt, and others—signed significant legislation or issued executive orders that protected the American natural environment by establishing forest preserves and wildlife refuges. The Civilian Conservation Corps was established by Franklin Roosevelt in 1933. In 1955, President Eisenhower signed into law the Air Pollution Control Act, which was later strengthened by the Clean Air Act of 1963, signed by President Lyndon Johnson. President Richard Nixon established the Environmental Protection Agency in 1970 and signed the Marine Mammal Protection Act in 1972, the Clean Water Act in 1972, and the Endangered Species Act in 1973. State governments followed the federal lead by establishing departments of environmental management to monitor and protect natural landscapes. Local governments have also become involved in protecting natural environments. The Yosemite Valley Grant Act, which Lincoln signed during the Civil War, was the forerunner of these governmental initiatives to protect the natural environment.

The federal government's management of the American environment has not always been harmless, and environmental threats, especially the prospect of worldwide climate change, are ongoing. But the nonmanagement model in place before Lincoln assumed the presidency would likely have resulted in more environmental damage during the century and a half since he served. Some recent environmental improvements are worth noting. Rhode Island's Blackstone River was dammed in 1790 and severely polluted by the factories lining its banks and by raw sewage through the 1960s. The Blackstone will never return to its pristine pre-1790 state, but it is now clean enough to be stocked with trout by the Rhode Island Department of Environmental Management. It has become a destination for fishermen, canoeists, and kayakers seeking a day of recreation on a scenic river. The Clean Water Act and the closing of factories along rivers have helped restore many previously polluted rivers. A 2016 article in the *New York Times* reported that after more than a century and a half, the Penobscot River in Maine, dammed in the 1830s to power a mill and undammed in 2012 and 2013, has seen a return of salmon swimming upstream to reach fresh water and spawn.[9] Had Henry David Thoreau lived to celebrate his two hundredth birthday in July 2017, he would surely have cheered this development.

In *Nature*, Ralph Waldo Emerson wrote, "The poet, the orator, bred in the woods, . . . shall not lose their lesson altogether, in the roar of cities or the broil of politics."[10] Lincoln was bred in the woods, and through most of his adult life, he was immersed in the broil of politics. He began his life trying to tame nature—to cut farm fields out of dense forests, to survive and eke out a living in a harsh and often unforgiving natural environment. He began his political career as a member of a political party that tried to master the environment with internal improvement projects—to connect two bodies of water with a canal, to build railroads that cut through wilderness areas, for example. As president, however, Lincoln, along with Congress, put into place some policies and practices that helped preserve the forests and other elements of the natural landscape, and those efforts set a precedent for future presidents to do the same.

ACKNOWLEDGMENTS

I would like to thank the editors of the Concise Lincoln Library of Southern Illinois University Press, Sylvia Frank Rodrigue and Richard Etulain, for their initial interest in a book on Abraham Lincoln and the natural environment and for their sustained support throughout the project. They were encouraging, patient, and critical in a very positive and helpful way; they provided the exact editorial assistance that I needed. I also appreciate the comments and suggestions offered by an anonymous scholar who reviewed my manuscript.

I acknowledge support from the Roger Williams University Foundation to Promote Scholarship and Teaching (RWU FPST). Over the past several years, the RWU FPST has provided me with several course-release grants to develop scholarly topics, including this one.

The inspiration for this book comes from a variety of sources: John Barrett, my high school biology teacher, who included a unit on ecology in a course in advanced biology in 1971 at Paul VI High School in Clifton, New Jersey; my brother, George Tackach, who taught me the art of fly fishing twenty-five years ago, which resulted in my experiencing some of the most environmentally pleasing places in the United States—the Yellowstone River, the Shenandoah River, Schoharie Creek in the Catskill Mountains, and the Wood and Narrow Rivers in Rhode Island; my biology colleagues at Roger Williams University, Scott Rutherford, Loren Byrne, Andy Rhyne, Dale Leavitt, and Paul Webb, whose lunchtime discussions with an English professor on environmental matters prompted me to write a book on the environment; and the many fine Lincoln scholars with whom I have come in contact since I began writing about Lincoln eighteen years ago, especially the members of the Lincoln Group of Boston.

NOTES

Introduction

1. Lincoln, "Second Inaugural Address," March 4, 1865, *Collected Works*, 8:333. The documents in *The Collected Works of Abraham Lincoln* contain occasional spelling or punctuation errors. Rather than correcting these errors or signaling them with "[*sic*]," we have left them as they appear in the original.
2. Bryce, "America's Greenest Presidents."
3. Gunther, "6 Eco-Friendly Presidents."
4. "Best and Worst Green Presidents."
5. Merchant, "Top 10 Greenest US Presidents."
6. Graham, *Presidents and the American Environment*, 25–29, 114–327, 16.
7. See Fiege, *Republic of Nature*, 159–247; Fraysse, *Lincoln, Land, and Labor*.

1. I Was Raised to Farm Work

1. Lincoln, "To Jesse W. Fell, Enclosing Autobiography," December 20, 1859, *Collected Works*, 3:511–12.
2. Marx, *Machine in the Garden*, 115.
3. See Winkle, *Young Eagle*, 3–4, or Donald, *Lincoln*, 19, for a detailed account of the Lincoln family's migration.
4. Worster, *Wealth of Nature*, 9–10; Steinberg, *Down to Earth*, 40; Merchant, *American Environmental History*, 35.
5. Miller, *Lincoln and His World: The Early Years*, 33–35.
6. Lincoln, "Autobiography Written for John L. Scripps," ca. June 1860, *Collected Works*, 4:62.
7. John L. Scripps to William H. Herndon, June 24, 1865, as cited in Wilson and Davis, *Herndon's Informants*, 57.
8. Rice, *Reminiscences of Abraham Lincoln*, 69.
9. Miller, *Lincoln and His World: The Early Years*, 62.
10. The Irish potato famine of the 1840s would vividly testify to the environmental vulnerability that farming communities faced. A fungus that attached itself to potato plants caused mass starvation among farmers in Ireland whose diet depended on potatoes.
11. Steinberg, *Down to Earth*, 10.
12. Memorandum of a statement by J. J. Wright, April 18, 1896, as cited in Fehrenbacher and Fehrenbacher, *Recollected Words of Abraham Lincoln*, 508.

13. Blumenthal, *Self-Made Man*, 26.
14. Shenk, *Lincoln's Melancholy*, 4, 13; Gienapp, *Abraham Lincoln and Civil War America*, 4; Donald, *Lincoln*, 27; Blumenthal, *Self-Made Man*, 6–7.
15. Winkle, *Young Eagle*, 14.
16. Donald, *Lincoln*, 33; White, *A. Lincoln*, 30; Fiege, *Republic of Nature*, 161; Winger, *Lincoln, Religion, and Romantic Cultural Politics*, 55; Gienapp, *Abraham Lincoln and Civil War America*, 3; Wilson, *Honor's Voice*, 57; Miller, *Lincoln and His World: The Early Years*, 63; Burlingame, *Abraham Lincoln*, 44–45.
17. Burlingame, *Inner World of Abraham Lincoln*, 37; Fiege, *Republic of Nature*, 162; Blumenthal, *Self-Made Man*, 3.
18. Miller, *Lincoln and His World: The Early Years*, 18.
19. Bray, *Reading with Lincoln*, 1.
20. Gen. 3:19.
21. Lincoln, "First Lecture on Discoveries and Inventions," April 6, 1858, *Collected Works*, 2:440.
22. Shenk, *Lincoln's Melancholy*, 17.
23. Lincoln, "Autobiography Written for John L. Scripps," ca. June 1860, *Collected Works*, 4:61.
24. Current, *Lincoln Nobody Knows*, 24.
25. Miller, *Lincoln and His World: The Early Years*, 69; Blumenthal, *Self-Made Man*, 34–35.
26. Thomas, *Abraham Lincoln*, 17; Blumenthal, *Self-Made Man*, 44.
27. Miller, *Lincoln and His World: The Early Years*, 81.
28. Twain, *Life on the Mississippi*, 10.
29. Miller, *Lincoln and His World: The Early Years*, 91–94.
30. Ibid., 98–99.
31. Shenk, *Lincoln's Melancholy*, 20–21.
32. Frayssé, *Lincoln, Land, and Labor*, 34.
33. Blumenthal, *Self-Made Man*, 3–5.
34. Shenk, *Lincoln's Melancholy*, 27.
35. Miller, *Lincoln and His World: The Early Years*, 112.
36. Donald, *Lincoln*, 71; Blumenthal, *Self-Made Man*, 56.
37. Miller, *Lincoln and His World: The Early Years*, 128–32.
38. Lincoln, "Communication to the People of Sangamo County," March 9, 1832, *Collected Works*, 1:5–7.
39. Donald, *Lincoln*, 45.
40. Miller, *Lincoln and His World: The Early Years*, 123.
41. Donald, *Lincoln*, 67.
42. Lincoln, "To Joshua F. Speed," March 27, 1842, *Collected Works*, 1:282.
43. Frayssé, *Lincoln, Land, and Labor*, 51.

44. Carwardine, *Lincoln*, 5; Shenk, *Lincoln's Melancholy*, 15; Gienapp, *Abraham Lincoln and Civil War America*, 11; Winkle, *Young Eagle*, 132.

45. Johnston, "John D. Johnston to Abraham Lincoln"; Chapman, "Augustus H. Chapman to Abraham Lincoln."

46. Lincoln, "To John D. Johnston," January 12, 1851, *Collected Works*, 2:97.

47. Herndon, *Life of Lincoln*, 387–88.

48. Tackach, *Historic Homes of America*, 134–37.

2. Internal Improvements

1. Jefferson, *Notes on the State of Virginia*, 164–65.

2. Hamilton, *Hamilton's Report on the Subject of Manufactures, 1791*.

3. Magoc, *Chronology of Americans and the Environment*, 10.

4. Merchant, *Columbia Guide to American Environmental History*, 29.

5. Merchant, *American Environmental History*, 112; Magoc, *Chronology of Americans and the Environment*, 26.

6. Marx, *Machine in the Garden*, 149.

7. Merchant, *American Environmental History*, 68.

8. Magoc, *Chronology of Americans and the Environment*, 24.

9. Marx, *Machine in the Garden*, 215.

10. Lincoln, "Seventh and Last Debate with Stephen A. Douglas at Alton, Illinois," October 15, 1858, *Collected Works*, 3:309.

11. Shabecoff, *Fierce Green Fire*, 26.

12. Albert Gallatin, "A Report on Roads and Canals," April 6, 1808, quoted in Merchant, *American Environmental History*, 68.

13. Brady, *War upon the Land*, 31.

14. Andrews, *Managing the Environment*, 89.

15. Miller, *Lincoln and His World: Prairie Politician*, 17.

16. Lincoln, "Bill Introduced in Illinois Legislature to Authorize Samuel Musick to Build a Toll Bridge," December 15, 1834, *Collected Works*, 1:29–30.

17. William Herndon interview with Joshua F. Speed, quoted in Wilson and Davis, *Herndon's Informants*, 476.

18. Lincoln, "Remarks in the Illinois Legislature Concerning the Illinois and Michigan Canals," January 22, 23, 1840, *Collected Works*, 1:196.

19. Lincoln, "Report and Resolutions in Relation to Purchase of Public Lands," January 17, 1839, *Collected Works*, 1:135–36.

20. Lincoln, "Report on Alton and Springfield Railroad," August 5, 1847, *Collected Works*, 1:398.

21. Lincoln, "Speech in the United States House of Representatives on Internal Improvements," June 20, 1848, *Collected Works*, 1:480–90.

22. Lincoln, "Application for Patent on an Improved Method of Lifting Vessels over Shoals," March 10, 1849, *Collected Works*, 2:33.

23. White, *A. Lincoln*, 209–10; Donald, *Lincoln*, 154, 168–69; Burlingame, *Abraham Lincoln*, 334–35.

24. Lincoln, "Annual Message to Congress," December 1, 1862, *Collected Works*, 5:526.

25. Lincoln, "Campaign Circular from Whig Committee," March 4, 1843, *Collected Works*, 1:310.

26. Ibid.

27. Lincoln, "First Lecture on Discoveries and Inventions," April 6, 1858, *Collected Works*, 2:437.

28. Lincoln, "Second Lecture on Discoveries and Inventions," February 11, 1859, *Collected Works*, 3:363.

29. Lincoln, "Address before the Wisconsin State Agricultural Society, Milwaukee, Wisconsin," September 30, 1859, *Collected Works*, 3:476–77.

30. See Wheeler, *Mr. Lincoln's T-Mails*.

31. Lincoln, "To Edward Wallace," October 11, 1859, *Collected Works*, 3:487.

32. Lincoln, "Speech at Pittsburgh, Pennsylvania," February 15, 1861, *Collected Works*, 4:213.

33. Marx, *Machine in the Garden*, 18.

34. Kulik, "Dams, Fish, and Farmers: Defense of Public Rights in Eighteenth-Century Rhode Island," 25–50; Steinberg, *Down to Earth*, 57.

35. Steinberg, *Down to Earth*, 56–58.

36. Merchant, *American Environmental History*, 124.

37. Buell, *Environmental Imagination*, 115.

38. Thoreau, *Week on the Concord and Merrimack Rivers*, 155–56, 159.

39. Steinberg, *Down to Earth*, 58.

40. In his list of books that Lincoln likely read, Robert Bray names none authored by Henry David Thoreau. See *Reading with Lincoln*, 223–29.

41. Merchant, *American Environmental History*, 51.

42. Magoc, *Chronology of Americans and the Environment*, 25.

43. Andrews, *Managing the Environment*, 39.

44. Shabecoff, *Fierce Green Fire*, 27–28.

45. Thoreau, "Walking," 627.

46. Sachs, "Stumps in the Wilderness," 100.

47. "Trip to Vermont," *Harbinger* 5, no. 4 (July 1847): 52.

48. Fiege, *Republic of Nature*, 243.

49. Ibid., 247.

50. Merchant, *American Environmental History*, 69.

51. Thoreau, *Walden*, 78.

3. My Childhood-Home I See Again

1. Lincoln, "To Andrew Johnston," February 24, 1846, *Collected Works*, 1:367.

2. Lincoln, "My Childhood-Home I See Again," [February 25?] 1846, *Collected Works*, 1:367–70. A second version of the poem's fourth line reads, "There's pleasure in it too." See "To Andrew Johnson," April 18, 1846, *Collected Works*, 1:378.

3. Barrett, "Abraham Lincoln's Poetry," 30–31, 33.

4. Fiege, *Republic of Nature*, 167.

5. Herndon, *Life of Lincoln*, 238–39.

6. Lincoln, "Fragment: Niagara Falls," ca. September 25–30, 1848, *Collected Works*, 2:10–11.

7. John Hanks interview with William H. Herndon, quoted in Wilson and Davis, *Herndon's Informants*, 455.

8. Joseph Gillespie to William H. Herndon, January 31, 1866, quoted in Wilson and Davis, *Herndon's Informants*, 182, 187.

9. William H. Herndon to Jesse W. Weik (undated), quoted in Fehrenbacher and Fehrenbacher, *Recollected Words of Abraham Lincoln*, 239; Richardson, *Secret Service*, 314–15.

10. Robert Livingston Stanton, "Reminiscences of President Lincoln," ca. 1883, quoted in Fehrenbacher and Fehrenbacher, *Recollected Words of Abraham Lincoln*, 265.

11. Rice, *Reminiscences of Abraham Lincoln*, 400.

12. Diary of George Templeton Strong, January 28, 1862, quoted in Fehrenbacher and Fehrenbacher, *Recollected Words of Abraham Lincoln*, 430.

13. Lincoln, "Address before the Young Men's Lyceum of Springfield, Illinois," January 27, 1838, *Collected Works*, 1:109, 112.

14. Ibid., 1:113–15.

15. Lincoln, "Speech at Chicago, Illinois," July 10, 1858, *Collected Works*, 2:492.

16. Lincoln, "To Mary Speed," September 27, 1841, *Collected Works*, 1:260.

17. Lincoln, "Address at Sanitary Fair, Baltimore, Maryland," April 18, 1864, *Collected Works*, 7:301–2.

18. Lincoln, "Autobiography Written for John L. Scripps," ca. June 1860, *Collected Works*, 4:67.

19. Lincoln, "Editorial on the Kansas-Nebraska Act," September 11, 1854, *Collected Works*, 2:230.

20. Lincoln, "Speech at Springfield, Illinois," October 4, 1854, *Collected Works*, 2:242.

21. Lincoln, "To Joseph Hooker," June 5, 1863, *Collected Works*, 6:249; "To Joseph Hooker," June 14, 1863, *Collected Works*, 6:273.

22. Lincoln, "To Oliver O. Howard," July 21, 1863, *Collected Works*, 6:341.

23. Lincoln, "To Charles D. Drake and Others," October 5, 1863, *Collected Works*, 6:500.

24. Lincoln, "Second Inaugural Address," March 4, 1865, *Collected Works*, 8:333.
25. Wills, "David Wills to Abraham Lincoln."
26. Lincoln, "Address Delivered at the Dedication of the Cemetery at Gettysburg," Final Text, November 19, 1863, *Collected Works*, 7:23.
27. Boritt, *Gettysburg Gospel*, 120; Wills, *Lincoln at Gettysburg*, 172.
28. Pinsker, *Lincoln's Sanctuary*, 1, 5.
29. Brownstein, *Lincoln's Other White House*, 13–15, 53–54; White, *A. Lincoln*, 488; Conroy, *Lincoln's White House*, 105–8.
30. *Washington Sunday Chronicle*, April 14, 1861, quoted in Pinsker, *Lincoln's Sanctuary*, 2.
31. John Hay's Civil War diary, August 23, 1863, quoted in Burlingame and Ettlinger, *Inside Lincoln's White House*, 75–76.
32. Carpenter, *Inner Life of Abraham Lincoln*, 223–25.
33. Bray, *Reading with Lincoln*, 106–7, 114–15.
34. Byron, *Childe Harold's Pilgrimage*, 82.
35. Blumenthal, *Self-Made Man*, 345.
36. Huth, "Aesthetic Emphasis," 28; Miller, *Central Park*, 74.
37. Bryant, "Inscription for the Entrance to a Wood," 126.
38. Bray, *Reading with Lincoln*, 227–28.
39. Parkman, *Oregon Trail*, 281.
40. Emerson, *Nature*, 34.
41. Bray, *Reading with Lincoln*, 225.

4. This Mighty Scourge of War

1. Lincoln, "Remarks at Springfield, Illinois," November 20, 1860, *Collected Works*, 4:142–43; "Speech at Pittsburgh, Pennsylvania," February 15, 1861, *Collected Works*, 4:211; "Speech at Independence Hall, Philadelphia," February 22, 1861, *Collected Works*, 4:240–41; "Reply to Governor Andrew J. Curtin at Harrisburg, Pennsylvania," February 22, 1861, *Collected Works*, 4:243.
2. Lincoln, "First Inaugural Address—Final Text," March 4, 1861, *Collected Works*, 4:265, 271.
3. Lincoln, "Message to Congress in Special Session," July 4, 1861, *Collected Works*, 4:431.
4. Sherman, *Memoirs*, 195.
5. Perrett, *Lincoln's War*, 66.
6. Current, *Lincoln Nobody Knows*, 136; Perrett, *Lincoln's War*, 52–53.
7. Sherman, *Memoirs*, 199.
8. Kennett, *Sherman*, 221–22.
9. Bray, *Reading with Lincoln*, 225.

10. Gienapp, *Abraham Lincoln and Civil War America*, 87, 99–101.

11. McClellan, "George B. McClellan to Abraham Lincoln."

12. Sherman, *Memoirs*, 298.

13. William T. Sherman to Leslie Coombs, August 1, 1864, quoted in Kennett, *Sherman*, 224–27.

14. James Dixon to Leonard Bacon, December 26, 1860, quoted in Royster, *Destructive War*, 79.

15. Nelson, *Ruin Nation*, 34.

16. McPherson, *Crossroads of Freedom*, 3.

17. Royster, *Destructive War*, 85–89; Brady, *War upon the Land*, 70–78.

18. William T. Sherman to Ulysses S. Grant, telegraph, July 18, 1863, quoted in Brady, *War upon the Land*, 68.

19. William T. Sherman to Salmon Chase, August 10, 1862, and William T. Sherman to Horatio Wright, September 20, 1862, quoted in Kennett, *Sherman*, 230.

20. Sherman, *Memoirs*, 585, 601.

21. White, *A. Lincoln*, 658.

22. Harris, *Lincoln's Last Months*, 49.

23. Donald, *Lincoln*, 514.

24. Sherman, *Memoirs*, 655, 627–29.

25. Royster, *Destructive War*, 30.

26. Brady, *War upon the Land*, 90, 84.

27. Lincoln, "Order of Thanks to William T. Sherman," September 3, 1864, *Collected Works*, 7:533; "Proclamation of Thanksgiving and Prayer," September 3, 1864, *Collected Works*, 7:533; "To William T. Sherman," December 26, 1864, *Collected Works*, 8:181–82; "Response to a Serenade," March 3, 1865, *Collected Works*, 8:331.

28. Nelson, *Ruin Nation*, 32.

29. Lincoln, "Second Inaugural Address," March 4, 1865, *Collected Works*, 8:332–33.

30. Sutter, "Epilogue," 231; Widmer, "Civil War's Environmental Impact," 326; Kirby, "American Civil War," part 1.

31. Sutter, "Epilogue," 232; Johnson, "Reconstructing the Soil," 195.

32. Nelson, *Ruin Nation*, 104–52.

33. Brady, *War upon the Land*, 122–23, 113.

34. Charles Morse to His Mother, March 28, 1862, quoted in Nelson, *Ruin Nation*, 146.

35. Widmer, "Civil War's Environmental Impact," 327.

36. Rhodes, *All for the Union*, 213.

37. Sachs, "Stumps in the Wilderness," 100.

38. Starr, "American Forests," 215.

39. Nelson, *Ruin Nation*, 152.

40. Widmer, "Civil War's Environmental Impact," 329; Kirby, "American Civil War," part 2.

41. Sherman, *Memoirs*, 656; Brady, *War upon the Land*, 95.

42. Ward, Burns, and Burns, *Civil War*, 184.

43. Fiege, *Republic of Nature*, 193.

44. Wills, *Lincoln at Gettysburg*, 19–40.

45. Small, "From Samuel Small to Abraham Lincoln."

46. Doughty, "From John W. Doughty to Abraham Lincoln."

47. Bruce, *Lincoln and the Tools of War*, 248.

48. For a detailed study of the chemical weaponry proposed during the Civil War, see Hasegawa, *Villainous Compounds*.

49. Kirby, "American Civil War," part 2.

50. Lowenthal, introduction to *Man and Nature*, xxv.

51. Bierce, *Civil War Short Stories*, 120.

52. Steinberg, *Down to Earth*, 99.

53. Faulkner, *Sound and the Fury*, 372.

54. Kirby, "American Civil War," part 4; Sachs, "Stumps in the Wilderness," 103; Sutter, "Epilogue," 231.

5. The Fruitful Source of Advantage to All Our People

1. Buell, *Writing for an Endangered World*, 2.

2. Melville, "Bartleby, the Scrivener," 46.

3. See Louv, *Last Child in the Woods*.

4. Sachs, "Stumps in the Wilderness," 103–4; Wills, *Lincoln at Gettysburg*, 63–65.

5. Miller, "Fate of Wilderness in American Landscape Art," 93; Novak, *Nature and Culture*, 161–63.

6. Cole, "Lament of the Forest," 230–32, 235.

7. Hickman, "How a Giant Tree's Death Sparked the Conservation Movement."

8. Graham, *Presidents and the American Environment*, 5.

9. Catlin, "Artist Proposes a National Park," 9.

10. Thoreau, *Maine Woods*, 684–85, 712. The article "Chesuncook," first published in the *Atlantic Monthly*, was included in *The Maine Woods*, published after Thoreau's death.

11. Philipon, *Conserving Words*, 125.

12. Sachs, *Humboldt Current*, 209.

13. Worster, *Wealth of Nature*, 102; Fraysse, *Lincoln, Land, and Labor*, 145.

14. Lincoln, "Speech to Germans at Cincinnati, Ohio," February 12, 1861, *Collected Works*, 4:202; Lincoln, "Annual Message to Congress," December 8, 1863," *Collected Works*, 7:46.

15. Contemporary U.S. presidents such as Jimmy Carter and Barack Obama have received high marks from environmentalists for preserving millions of acres federal land from development and keeping that land in the public domain for recreation and appreciation.

16. Lincoln, "To the Senate and House of Representatives," July 19, 1861, *Collected Works*, 4:453–54. In the summer of 1861, Congress was likely not eager to conduct business with Great Britain. The British were angry with the Lincoln administration's blockade of the South's ports because Southern cotton was needed for Great Britain's textile mills. The British were considering recognizing the Confederacy's independence.

17. Etulain, *Lincoln and Oregon Country*, 3.

18. Mackie, "Lincoln and the California Connections," 151–52.

19. Yosemite Valley Grant Act, U.S.C., title 16, sec. 48.

20. Spirm, "Constructing Nature," 92; Johnson, "Wilderness Parks and Their Discontents," 114.

21. Olmsted, "Great Glory of Nature," 305, 307–8.

22. Lincoln, "Annual Message to Congress," December 3, 1861, *Collected Works*, 5:46.

23. Lincoln, "Annual Message to Congress," December 1, 1862, *Collected Works*, 5:526–27.

24. Starr, "American Forests," 220.

25. Lincoln, "Address Delivered at the Dedication of the Cemetery at Gettysburg," November 19, 1863, *Collected Works*, 7:23.

26. Sutter, "Epilogue," 234.

27. Bray, *Reading with Lincoln*, 229.

28. Mentor Graham to William H. Herndon, July 15, 1865, quoted in Wilson and Davis, *Herndon's Informants*, 76; Robert B. Rutledge to William H. Herndon, November 30, 1866, quoted in ibid., 426.

29. Herndon, *Life of Lincoln*, 353–54.

30. Tyson, "Lincoln Seedbed," 189.

31. Lowenthal, introduction to *Man and Nature*, xvii–xviii.

32. Marsh, *Man and Nature*, 3, 36, 187.

33. Merchant, *American Environmental History*, 142.

34. Keckley, *Behind the Scenes*, 169–70. The last name of the author of *Behind the Scenes* is sometimes spelled Keckly. The spelling used here, Keckley, is the one appearing on the cover of *Behind the Scenes*.

Epilogue

1. Andrews, *Managing the Environment*, x.

2. "Historical Timeline: Farmers & the Land."

3. Nickerson, "New England Sees a Return of Forests, Wildlife."

4. Carson, *Silent Spring*, 157–58, 162–69.

5. Lincoln, "Second Inaugural Address," March 4, 1865, *Collected Works*, 8:333.

6. Kirby, "American Civil War," part 4.

7. Graham, *Presidents and the Environment*, 1, 9, 19.

8. Ibid., 1.

9. Carpenter, "Letting the Fish Flow Anew," D6.

10. Emerson, *Nature*, 34.

BIBLIOGRAPHY

Andrews, Richard N. L. *Managing the Environment, Managing Ourselves: A History of American Environmental Politics.* New Haven, CT: Yale University Press, 1999.

Barrett, Faith. "Abraham Lincoln's Poetry." In *The Cambridge Companion to Abraham Lincoln*, edited by Shirley Samuels, 22–39. New York: Cambridge University Press, 2012.

"The Best and Worst Green Presidents." *Autonomie Project* (blog). June 30, 2009. https://autonomieproject.wordpress.com/2009/06/30/the-best-and-worst-green-presidents.

Bierce, Ambrose. *The Civil War Short Stories of Ambrose Bierce.* Edited by Ernest J. Hopkins. Lincoln: University of Nebraska Press, 1970.

Blumenthal, Sidney. *A Self-Made Man: The Political Life of Abraham Lincoln, 1809–1849.* New York: Simon and Schuster, 2016.

Bode, Carl, ed. *The Portable Thoreau.* Rev. ed. New York: Viking Press, 1964.

Boritt, Gabor. *The Gettysburg Gospel: The Lincoln Speech That Nobody Knows.* New York: Simon and Schuster, 2006.

Brady, Lisa. *War upon the Land: Military Strategy and the Transformation of Southern Landscape during the American Civil War.* Athens: University of Georgia Press, 2012.

Bray, Robert. *Reading with Lincoln.* Carbondale: Southern Illinois University Press, 2010.

Brownstein, Elizabeth Smith. *Lincoln's Other White House: The Untold Story of the Man and His Presidency.* Hoboken, NJ: John Wiley and Sons, 2005.

Bruce, Robert V. *Lincoln and the Tools of War.* Indianapolis: Bobbs-Merrill, 1956.

Bryant, William Cullen. "Inscription for the Entrance to a Wood." In Hollander, *American Poetry*, 126–27.

Bryce, Emma. "America's Greenest Presidents." *New York Times* (blog). September 20, 2012. http://green.blogs.nytimes.com/2012/09/20/americas-greenest-presidents/?_r=0.

Buell, Lawrence. *The Environmental Imagination: Thoreau, Nature Writing, and the Formation of American Culture.* Cambridge, MA: Belknap Press, 1995.

———. *Writing for an Endangered World: Literature, Culture and Environment in the United States and Beyond.* Cambridge, MA: Belknap Press, 2001.

Burlingame, Michael. *Abraham Lincoln: A Life.* 2 vols. Baltimore: John Hopkins Press, 2008.

———. *The Inner World of Abraham Lincoln.* Urbana: University of Illinois Press, 1994.

Burlingame, Michael, and John R. Turner Ettlinger, eds. *Inside Lincoln's White House: The Complete Civil War Diary of John Hay.* Carbondale: Southern Illinois University Press, 1997.

Byron, George Gordon. *Childe Harold's Pilgrimage.* 1812–18. In *Byron's Poetry*, edited by Frank D. McConnell, 24–84. New York: W. W. Norton, 1978.

Carpenter, F. B. *The Inner Life of Abraham Lincoln.* 1866. Reprint, Lincoln: University of Nebraska Press, 1995.

Carpenter, Murray. "Letting the Fish Flow Anew." *New York Times*, October 25, 2016, D6.

Carson, Rachel. *Silent Spring.* 1962. Reprint, Boston: Houghton Mifflin, 2002.

Carwardine, Richard. *Lincoln: A Life of Purpose and Power.* New York: Alfred A. Knopf, 2006.

Catlin, George. "An Artist Proposes a National Park." In *The American Environment: Readings in the History of Conservation*, edited by Roderick Nash, 5–9. Reading, MA: Addison-Wesley, 1968.

Chapman, Augustus H. "Augustus H. Chapman to Abraham Lincoln," May 24, 1849. In *The Abraham Lincoln Papers at the Library of Congress*, https://www.loc.gov/item/mal0033700/.

Cole, Thomas. "The Lament of the Forest." In Hollander, *American Poetry*, 230–35.

Conroy, James B. *Lincoln's White House: The People's House in Wartime.* Lanham, MD: Rowman and Littlefield, 2017.

Current, Richard N. *The Lincoln Nobody Knows.* New York: Hill and Wang, 1958.

Donald, David. *Lincoln.* New York: Simon and Schuster, 1995.

Doughty, John W. "John W. Doughty to Abraham Lincoln," May 1, 1862. RG 156, Entry 994: Miscellaneous Records, Ordnance Department Special File, 1812–1912, Correspondence Relating to Inventions, 1812–1870, NAB. https://s3.us-east-2.amazonaws.com/papersofabrahamlincoln/PAL_Images/PAL_PubMan/1862/05/275642.pdf.

Drake, Brian, ed. *The Blue, the Gray, and the Green: Toward an Environmental History of the Civil War.* Athens: University of Georgia Press, 2015.

Emerson, Ralph Waldo. *Nature.* 1836. In *Selections from Ralph Waldo Emerson*, edited by Stephen E. Whicher, 23–56. Boston: Houghton Mifflin, 1957.

Etulain, Richard W. *Lincoln and Oregon Country: Politics in the Civil War Era.* Corvallis: Oregon State University Press, 2013.

Faulkner, William. *The Sound and the Fury.* New York: Vintage Books, 1929.

Fehrenbacher, Don E., and Virginia Fehrenbacher, eds. *Recollected Words of Abraham Lincoln.* Stanford, CA: Stanford University Press, 1996.

Fiege, Mark. *The Republic of Nature: An Environmental History of the United States*. Seattle: University of Washington Press, 2012.

Frayssé, Olivier. *Lincoln, Land, and Labor: 1809–60*. Translated by Sylvia Neely. Urbana: University of Illinois Press, 1988.

Gienapp, William E. *Abraham Lincoln and Civil War America*. New York: Oxford University Press, 2002.

Graham, Otis L., Jr. *Presidents and the American Environment*. Lawrence: University Press of Kansas, 2015.

Gunther, Shea. "6 Eco-Friendly Presidents." February 21, 2011. http://www.mnn.com/earth-matters/politics/photos/6-eco-friendly-presidents/green-white-house-residents.

Hamilton, Alexander. *Hamilton's Report on the Subject of Manufactures, 1791*. *History Now*, Gilder Lehrman Institute of American History. https://www.gilderlehrman.org/content/hamilton%E2%80%99s-report-subject-manufactures-1791.

Harris, William C. *Lincoln's Last Months*. Cambridge, MA: Belknap Press, 2004.

Hasegawa, Guy. *Villainous Compounds: Chemical Weapons and the American Civil War*. Carbondale: Southern Illinois University Press, 2015.

Herndon, William H. *Life of Lincoln*. 1888. Reprint, Cleveland: Fine Editions Press, 1949.

Hickman, Leo. "How a Giant Tree's Death Sparked the Conservation Movement 160 Years Ago." *Guardian*, June 27, 2013. https://www.theguardian.com/environment/blog/2013/jun27/giant-tree-death-conservation-movement.

"Historical Timeline: Farmers & the Land." Growing a Nation: The Story of American Agriculture. Last modified February 2, 2017. http://www.agclassroom.org/gan/timeline/farmers_land.htm.

Hollander, John, ed. *American Poetry: The Nineteenth Century*. Vol. 1, *Freneau to Whitman*. New York: Library of America, 1993.

Huth, Hans. "The Aesthetic Emphasis." In *Environment and Americans: The Problem of Priorities*, edited by Roderick Nash, 24–31. New York: Holt, Rinehart and Winston, 1972.

Jefferson, Thomas. *Notes on the State of Virginia*. 1787. Edited by William Peden. Reprint, Chapel Hill: University of North Carolina Press, 1954.

Johnson, Benjamin. "Wilderness Parks and Their Discontents." In Lewis, *American Wilderness*, 113–30.

Johnson, Timothy. "Reconstructing the Soil: Emancipation and the Roots of Chemical-Dependent Agricultural in America." In Drake, *The Blue, the Gray, and the Green*, 191–208.

Johnston, John D. "John D. Johnston to Abraham Lincoln." May 25, 1849. In *The Abraham Lincoln Papers at the Library of Congress*. https://www.loc.gov/item/mal0034000/.

Keckley, Elizabeth. *Behind the Scenes, or Thirty Years a Slave and Four Years in the White House.* New York: G. W. Carleton, 1868.

Kennett, Lee. *Sherman: A Soldier's Life.* New York: HarperCollins, 2001.

Kirby, Jack Temple. "The American Civil War: An Environmental View." *The Use of the Land: Perspectives on Stewardship.* National Humanities Center. Last modified July 2001. http://nationalhumanitiescenter.org /tserve/nattrans/ntuseland/essays/amcwar.htm.

Kulik, Gary. "Dams, Fish, and Farmers: Defense of Public Rights in Eighteenth-Century Rhode Island." In *The Countryside in the Age of Capitalist Transformation: Essays in the Social History of Rural America*, edited by Steven Hahn and Jonathan Prude, 25–50. Chapel Hill: University of North Carolina Press, 1985

Lewis, Michael, ed. *American Wilderness: A New History.* New York: Oxford University Press, 2007.

Lincoln, Abraham. *The Collected Works of Abraham Lincoln.* Edited by Roy P. Basler. 9 vols. New Brunswick, NJ: Rutgers University Press, 1953–1955.

Louv, Richard. *Last Child in the Woods: Saving Our Children from Nature-Deficit Disorder.* Chapel Hill, NC: Algonquin Books, 2005.

Lowenthal, David. Introduction to *Man and Nature, or Physical Geography as Modified by Human Affairs*, by George Perkins Marsh, ix–xxix. Edited by David Lowenthal. Cambridge, MA: Belknap Press, 1965.

Mackie, Thomas. "Lincoln and the California Connections." *Lincoln Herald* 116, no. 3 (Fall 2014): 149–53.

Magoc, Chris J. *Chronology of Americans and the Environment.* Santa Barbara, CA: ABC-CLIO, 2011.

Marsh, George Perkins. *Man and Nature, or Physical Geography as Modified by Human Affairs.* 1864. Reprint, Cambridge, MA: Belknap Press, 1965.

Marx, Leo. *The Machine in the Garden: Technology and the Pastoral Ideal in America.* New York: Oxford University Press, 1964.

McClellan, George B. "George B. McClellan to Abraham Lincoln." July 7, 1862. In *The Abraham Lincoln Papers at the Library of Congress.* https:// www.loc.gov/item/mal1683000/.

McPherson, James M. *Crossroads of Freedom: Antietam.* New York: Oxford University Press, 2002.

Melville, Herman. "Bartleby, the Scrivener: A Story of Wall Street." 1853. In *Great Short Works of Herman Melville*, edited by Warner Berthoff, 39–74. New York: Harper and Row, 1969.

Merchant, Brian. "The Top 10 Greenest US Presidents." *TreeHugger*, February 16, 2009. http://www.treehugger.com/corporate-responsibility/the -top-10-greenest-us-presidents.html.

Merchant, Carolyn. *American Environmental History: An Introduction.* New York: Columbia University Press, 2007.

———. *The Columbia Guide to American Environmental History.* New York: Columbia University Press, 2002.

Miller, Angela. "The Fate of Wilderness in American Landscape Art." In Lewis, *American Wilderness,* 91–112.

Miller, Richard Lawrence. *Lincoln and His World: The Early Years, Birth to Illinois Legislature.* Mechanicsburg, PA: Stackpole Books, 2006.

———. *Lincoln and His World: Prairie Politician, 1834–1842.* Mechanicsburg, PA: Stackpole Books, 2008.

Miller, Sara Cedar. *Central Park: An American Masterpiece.* New York: Harry N. Abrams, 2003.

Nelson, Megan Kate. *Ruin Nation: Destruction and the American Civil War.* Athens: University of Georgia Press, 2012.

Nickerson, Colin. "New England Sees a Return of Forests, Wildlife." *Boston Globe,* August 31, 2013. https://www.bostonglobe.com/metro/2013/08/31/new-england-sees-return-forests-and-wildlife/IJRxacv.

Novak, Barbara. *Nature and Culture: American Landscape and Painting, 1825–1875.* Rev. ed. New York: Oxford University Press, 1995.

Olmsted, Frederick Law. "The Greatest Glory of Nature: Preliminary Report upon the Yosemite and Big Tree Grove." 1865. In *Frederick Law Olmsted: Writing on Landscape, Culture and Society,* edited by Charles E. Beveridge, 300–318. New York: Library of America, 2015.

Parkman, Francis. *The Oregon Trail: Sketches of Prairie and Rocky-Mountain Life.* 1849. New York: Modern Library, 1949.

Perrett, Geoffrey. *Lincoln's War: The Untold Story of America's Greatest President as Commander in Chief.* New York: Random House, 2004.

Philipon, Daniel J. *Conserving Words: How American Nature Writers Shaped the Environmental Movement.* Athens: University of Georgia Press, 2004.

Pinsker, Matthew. *Lincoln's Sanctuary: Abraham Lincoln and the Soldiers' Home.* New York: Oxford University Press, 2003.

Rhodes, Robert Hunt, ed. *All for the Union: The Civil War Diary and Letters of Elisha Hunt Rhodes.* New York: Orion Books, 1985.

Rice, Allen Thorndike, ed. *Reminiscences of Abraham Lincoln by Distinguished Men of His Time.* 1885. Reprint, New York: Harper and Brothers, 1909.

Richardson, Albert D. *The Secret Service, the Field, the Dungeon, and the Escape.* Hartford, CT: American Publishing, 1865.

Royster, Charles. *The Destructive War: William Tecumseh Sherman, Stonewall Jackson, and the Americans.* New York: Alfred A. Knopf, 1991.

Sachs, Aaron. *The Humboldt Current: Nineteenth-Century Exploration and the Roots of American Environmentalism.* New York: Viking, 2006.

———. "Stumps in the Wilderness." In Drake, *The Blue, the Gray, and the Green*, 96–112.

Shabecoff, Philip. *A Fierce Green Fire: The American Environmental Movement.* Rev. ed. Washington: Island Press, 2003.

Shenk, Joshua Wolf. *Lincoln's Melancholy: How Depression Challenged a President and Fueled His Greatness.* Boston: Houghton Mifflin, 2005.

Sherman, William Tecumseh. *Memoirs of General W. T. Sherman.* 1875. New York: Library of America, 1990.

Small, Samuel. "Samuel Small to Abraham Lincoln." 1861. In *The Abraham Lincoln Papers at the Library of Congress.* https://www.loc.gov/item/mal0558300/.

Spirm, Anne Whiston. "Constructing Nature: The Legacy of Frederick Law Olmsted." In *Uncommon Ground: Toward Reinventing Nature*, edited by William Cronon, 91–113. New York: W. W. Norton, 1995

Starr, Frederick, Jr. "American Forests: Their Destruction and Preservation." In *Report of the Commissioner of Agriculture for the Year 1865*, 210–34. Washington, DC: U.S. Department of Agriculture, 1866.

Steinberg, Ted. *Down to Earth: Nature's Role in American History.* New York: Oxford University Press, 2002.

Sutter, Paul S. "Epilogue: 'Waving the Bloody Shirt.'" In Drake, *The Blue, the Gray, and the Green*, 225–35.

Tackach, James. *Historic Homes of America.* New York: Portland House, 1990.

Thomas, Benjamin. *Abraham Lincoln: A Biography.* 1952. New York: Modern Library, 1968.

Thoreau, Henry David. *The Maine Woods.* 1864. In *Thoreau*, edited by Robert F. Sayre, 590–845. New York: Library of America, 1985.

———. *Walden.* 1854. 2nd ed. New York: W. W. Norton, 1992.

———. "Walking." 1862. In Bode, *Portable Thoreau*, 592–630.

———. *A Week on the Concord and Merrimack Rivers.* 1849. In Bode, *Portable Thoreau*, 138–227.

"Trip to Vermont." *Harbinger* 5, no. 4 (July 1847): 52.

Twain, Mark. *Life on the Mississippi.* 1883. Reprint, New York: Bantam Books, 1981.

Tyson, Neil deGrasse. "The Lincoln Seedbed." In *The Gettysburg Replies: The World Responds to Abraham Lincoln's Gettysburg Address*, edited by Carla Knorowski, 188–89. Guilford, CT: Lyons Press, 2015

Ward, Geoffrey C., Ric Burns, and Ken Burns. *The Civil War: An Illustrated History.* New York: Knopf, 1990.

Wheeler, Tom. *Mr. Lincoln's T-Mails: How Abraham Lincoln Used the Telegraph to Win the Civil War.* New York: Harper Business, 2006.

White, Ronald C., Jr. *A. Lincoln: A Biography*. New York: Random House, 2009.

Widmer, Ted. "The Civil War's Environmental Impact." *New York Times*, November 15, 2014. In *The New York Times Disunion: A History of the Civil War*, edited by Ted Widmer, 326–31. New York: Oxford University Press, 2016.

Wills, David. "David Wills to Abraham Lincoln." November 2, 1863. In *The Abraham Lincoln Papers at the Library of Congress*. https://www.loc .gov/item/mal2778100/.

Wills, Garry. *Lincoln at Gettysburg: The Words That Remade America*. New York: Simon and Schuster, 1992.

Wilson, Douglas L. *Honor's Voice: The Transformation of Abraham Lincoln*. New York: Alfred A. Knopf, 1998.

Wilson, Douglas L., and Rodney O. Davis, eds. *Herndon's Informants: Letters, Interviews, and Statements about Abraham Lincoln*. Urbana: University of Illinois Press, 1998.

Winger, Stewart. *Lincoln, Religion, and Romantic Cultural Politics*. DeKalb: Northern Illinois University Press, 2003.

Winkle, Kenneth J. *Lincoln's Citadel: The Civil War in Washington, D.C.* New York: W. W. Norton, 2013.

———. *The Young Eagle: The Rise of Abraham Lincoln*. Dallas: Taylor Trade Publishing, 2001.

Worster, Donald. *The Wealth of Nature: Environmental History and the Ecological Imagination*. New York: Oxford University Press, 1993.

INDEX

Page numbers in italics indicate figures.

James Tackach, a professor of English at Roger Williams University in Bristol, Rhode Island, has authored *Lincoln's Moral Vision: The Second Inaugural Address* and, for young readers, *The Emancipation Proclamation: Abolishing Slavery in the South*. His articles on Abraham Lincoln and reviews of Lincoln books have appeared in *Lincoln: A President for the Ages*, the *Lincoln Herald*, *Studies in Puritan American Spirituality*, the *Register of the Kentucky Historical Society*, the *Journal of Illinois History*, the *Historian*, and *Foreign Policy*. His *Early Black Reformers* received the 2004 Carter G. Woodson Secondary Book Award, sponsored by the National Council for the Social Studies.

CONCISE
LINCOLN
LIBRARY

This series of concise books fills a need for short studies of the life, times, and legacy of President Abraham Lincoln. Each book gives readers the opportunity to quickly achieve basic knowledge of a Lincoln-related topic. These books bring fresh perspectives to well-known topics, investigate previously overlooked subjects, and explore in greater depth topics that have not yet received book-length treatment. For a complete list of current and forthcoming titles, see www.conciselincolnlibrary.com.

Other Books in the Concise Lincoln Library

Abraham Lincoln and Horace Greeley
Gregory A. Borchard

Lincoln and the Civil War
Michael Burlingame

Lincoln's Sense of Humor
Richard Carwardine

Lincoln and the Constitution
Brian R. Dirck

Lincoln in Indiana
Brian R. Dirck

Lincoln and the Election of 1860
Michael S. Green

Lincoln and Congress
William C. Harris

Lincoln and the Union Governors
William C. Harris

Lincoln and the Abolitionists
Stanley Harrold

Lincoln's Campaign Biographies
Thomas A. Horrocks

Lincoln and the Military
John F. Marszalek

Lincoln and Emancipation
Edna Greene Medford

Lincoln and Reconstruction
John C. Rodrigue

Lincoln and the Thirteenth Amendment
Christian G. Samito

Lincoln and Medicine
Glenna R. Schroeder-Lein

Lincoln and the Immigrant
Jason H. Silverman

Lincoln and the U.S. Colored Troops
John David Smith

Lincoln's Assassination
Edward Steers, Jr.

Lincoln and Race
Richard Striner

Lincoln and Religion
Ferenc Morton Szasz with Margaret Connell Szasz

Lincoln and the War's End
John C. Waugh

Lincoln as Hero
Frank J. Williams

Abraham and Mary Lincoln
Kenneth J. Winkle